WHO TOLD YOU
THAT YOU WERE NAKED?

WHO TOLD YOU
THAT YOU WERE NAKED?

Victor Schlatter

Destiny Image® Publishers, Inc.
P.O. Box 310
Shippensburg, PA 17257-0310

"Speaking to the Purposes of God for this Generation and for the Generations to Come."

For Worldwide Distribution, Printed in the U.S.A.

ISBN 10: 0-7684-2357-0
ISBN 13: 978-0-7684-2357-0

This book and all other Destiny Image, Revival Press, MercyPlace, Fresh Bread, Destiny Image Fiction, and Treasure House books are available at Christian bookstores and distributors worldwide.

For a U.S. bookstore nearest you, call
1-800-722-6774.

For more information on foreign distributors, call
717-532-3040.

Or reach us on the Internet:
www.destinyimage.com

1 2 3 4 5 6 7 8 9 10 11 / 09 08 07 06

DEDICATION

To no one else but **Abba**
whose plan it was—and whose conquest it will be!

A Good Verse to Keep in Mind...

I will rouse your sons, O Zion,
Against your sons, O Greece,
And make you like a warrior's sword
(Zechariah 9:13b).

...because it's an end-of-days promise that will be kept!

TABLE OF CONTENTS

INTRODUCTION

WHAT'S this book all about? It's like you've been driving in the early morning fog and it's a bit hard to see where you're going. Then the sun gradually gains predominance and the fog fades—it's a beautiful day in contrast to the way it seemed to start. Thus, we're going to see the fog lifting off a lot of things.

So it's about seeing it clearly after all.

And then it's like when everything seems not a little shaky all around you; but when all is said and done, there's more than enough bedrock far and wide for anyone who wants to stand up and stand tall.

So it's about hope after all.

And it also has its depth in Scripture—undoubtedly some Scripture that you may have never even noticed before. It's not about the scary stuff that many of the lads never got right in the first place, looking at it through glasses that focused anywhere from the spooky to the spectacular. I suggest those kind of spectacles be changed to contact lenses, and for starters you ought to be a bit familiar with the first three chapters of Genesis. That not only gives the setting for the air you breathe right now, but a panoramic view of the big picture.

So it's about understanding more about the *big why* after all.

And off and on, through the chapters, we'll meet a lady named Mrs. Adam's (don't forget to keep the apostrophe where it belongs), and her mischievous mentor, Slippery Sam. In fact I reckon we'd do well to call her to your attention on our front cover. Note, however, she's not whispering what most folks might think she's whispering, but we'll have to pick up on that later in the book.

Sam, on the other hand, is much of the problem but has nothing whatsoever to do with the solution. So at the end of the day (or the end of days), we can leave him tied in knots (or worse), which as you can imagine, significantly slows down his slithering.

And for sure, we'll pick up some excellent insights on nakedness—not the least, the painless prescription for such embarrassing exposures such as detailed ironically in the third chapters of both Genesis as well as Revelation, should you require any advance clues from your Consultant.

So let's move right on into the first Chapter regarding where we are at today, and why—and especially why—we need not worry, as Psalm 46 suggests: *"Therefore we will not fear, though the earth give way and the mountains fall into the heart of the sea, though its waters roar and foam and the mountains quake with their surging. There is a river whose streams make glad the city of God...."*

—Victor Schlatter
November 2005
Newe Oved, Israel

CHAPTER ONE

SLITHERING DOWN THE GARDEN PATH

I can think of no other verse in the entire Book of books that carries more significant prophetic punch from the dawn of creation until the curtain finally drops on the downfall of human experience than Genesis 3:5. So let's first put the whole scenario of those dim and misty doings of verse 5 into a clear picture:

> *Now the serpent was more crafty than any of the wild animals the Lord God had made. He said to the woman, "Did God really say, 'You must not eat from any tree in the garden'?" The woman said to the serpent, "We may eat fruit from the trees in the garden, but God did say, 'You must not eat fruit from the tree that is in the middle of the garden, and you must not touch it, or you will die.'" "You will not surely die," the serpent said to the woman. "For God knows when you eat of it your eyes will be opened, and you will be like God, knowing good and evil" (Genesis 3:1-5).*

As a sometime translator of Scripture into the worldview of a once Stone Age tribe of Papua New Guinea, I now find it equally fascinating to translate a bit of new truth into a global mind-set that has long been cast into the concrete of 21st-century materialism. So here is a rephrased version of how we might present the closer-to-home realities of our chummy Garden get-together above:

You're not going to die, Mrs. Adam's. [She belongs to Adam, of course, and I wouldn't rib you about that little detail.] *Look, the Big Man is holding out on you because He knows the minute you try it, you're going to be as clever as He is, and by then, you can steer your own ship just as well as He can—hey, Honey, maybe even better! Why don't you go ahead and try. You're too pretty to die!*

Now the Greek Hellenistic thinking with which we Westerners have all grown up, will plug that verse straight into the sex circuit, complete with the clichéd Adam's apple on which—according to traditional lore—her beloved nearly choked when she pulled him into her neat discovery in the shade of the Tree of New Ideas.

Sorry, but Genesis 3:5 has nothing to do with Greek-minded sex or Adam and Eve's intimate aspirations on Day One. The most historic Hebraic commentary on the Garden wedding is, *"...they were both naked...and were not ashamed"* (Gen. 2:25 KJV). The way the Creator God designed us male and female is, without question, His most unique architectural feat for procreation and continuity of life. And the purest!

The Good Book doesn't mention it, but I'm sure the Most High certainly would have won the Eden Prize in Creativity for that one. I enjoy disclosing this bit of brilliance to the disappointment of all of Charlie Darwin's cheering section who think that surfacing from a bit of bog slime is so magnificent. I suggest they go to a swamp to worship, but the problem is that there are no ATMs down there for the financially focused—only tadpoles. But the good news is there is still a day or so left for those who have been hoodwinked into a godless universe to come to their senses and recognize Intelligent Design along with that more than probable Garden Creativity Prize. How did we get off on to that?

Back to the sanctity of the design. It was the likes of the Canaanites, the Sodomites, and eventually the Hellenist nude gymnasiums that glorified not only the body, but the perversion of the Creator's most sacred physical presentation to humanity. On the other hand, to the ancient Hebraic mind, sexuality was a God-designed gift to be used in strict adherence to the Manufacturer's design, and that with thanksgiving to the Most High for His gracious gift. It was guaranteed for God's blessing and prosperity over tenure of up to 120 years, as in the case of Moses (see Deut. 34:7),[1] not to mention several other old-timers.

But if that forbidden fruit was not a flirtation with the flesh, as some of the old wives' tales would have it, what was it?

Well, throughout our time together in this book, we'll peek around a few fascinating corners and check into a reasonable number of other clandestine cupboards of history to check up on where all the seeds of that forbidden fruit might have fancied to fall. Certainly it would not have been too far from the tree, as another old cliché of wisdom will remind us.

Regardless, it's not a bad idea to bounce back to the biblical introduction of this Tree of Temptation that lists it merely as *"the tree of the knowledge of good and evil"* (Gen. 2:17), which points our thoughts neither toward promiscuity nor applesauce. Far closer to the matter are the impressive insights of the prophet Isaiah:

> *Woe to those who call evil good and good evil, who put darkness for light and light for darkness, who put bitter for sweet and sweet for bitter. Woe to those who are wise in their own eyes and clever in their own sight* (Isaiah 5:20-21).

Now that clues us in on the realities of good and evil far more than those other non-biblical pseudo presumptions that involve immoral sex or amoral Adam's apples! As for that clandestine whisper to her husband, Sammy the overgrown worm enticed them into a pickle, not an apple! And the Mother of all Humanism is off and running with some fresh ideas of how to fix it without outside interference from the Most High on down. Strike two!

Sadly, some 500 Christian sects, from stonewall fundamentalists to liquid-like liberals, vary in agreement as to what right and wrong might happen to consist of. And I almost forgot to mention a further multiplied number of morality measurements between good and evil among my esteemed rabbinical colleagues. The interpretations are legion. So there you are, back to square one—or perhaps better stated as *Tree One*. And all this comes from probing into the same pages of the same Book!

Perhaps the Good Rabbi from Galilee could help us here in one of His pertinent promises:

> *But when He, the Spirit of truth, comes, He will guide you into all truth. He will not speak on His own; He will speak only what He hears, and He will tell you what is yet to come* (John 16:13).

That text, sorry to say, may also have some problems in interpretation from one pulpit to the next as to who all may "theologically" have the privilege of hearing the *"still small voice."* That all depends, of course, on how clearly the preacher happens to know or hear the whisper himself. But in reality, that Voice should indeed cast an indelible shadow over any and all sectarian differences of ideas, *if* our bottom line is no more or no less than a deep yearning to hear from God.

Without question, the King of the Universe wants us to be like His Son, but it is certainly *not* by legalisms, competition, or pretense. Nor is it even by a well-intentioned effort to be a spiritual copycat, that is, in the vein of the sometime popular and catchy "What would Jesus do?" That's to use the head instead of the heart and come up grossly shortchanged. The Most High proposes not imitation, but implantation. He wants to reign and rule from within where His Spirit will politely *prompt us what to do*! He wants to fill us with Himself, with His divine breath, His *Ruach Ha Kodesh* (literally, "The Holy Breath" in Hebrew). And it is His Spirit that is the last word *to communicate good or evil to every member of His God-family*. And that's why He told Adam and Eve to steer clear of that tantalizing tree of temptation in the center of the Garden. "It's a

God-thing, Adam, so keep your distance; that one is not for you. It's My own command center!"

Before we go on, let's have one added look on the semantics of "being like God" from our opening text at the beginning of the chapter. Linguists and translators understand that the significance in word choice is not where two words *seem to be alike*, but key selection is *where they differ*. Nor are words defined only by digging into their root meanings, but just as meaningfully, into the context of their usage. And this is especially true when they hail from another culture or another era. Therefore, when Slithering Sammy hinted to Mama Eve that she would be *wise* (he didn't use that word, but that is what she had perceived in the following verse—see Gen. 3:6), our minds should catch that her human take on the concept was *clever* but certainly not *wise*. So much for a garden path!

May we now flow on into even more fascinating insights of the chapters to come. A tongue-in-cheek title for this book might have been, *The Chickens of Genesis 3:5 Come Home to Roost.* Unfortunately, from the initial attacks upon our Hebraic foundations some four centuries b.c., to the ensuing erosion of Judeo-Christian morality over the last two millennia, the people of promise have taken blow after blow after blow. Moreover, the avalanche of change over the last six decades alone has gravely revealed that the chickens are not only comfortably home and roosting, but as never before, doing their uttermost to dishonor, discredit, and bring disrepute upon the Father's family of redemption. We ought to be weighing what we're going to do next.

So let's begin to follow those seed trails from that desecrated Garden Grove all the way to modern humanism's Holy Grail of One-World Government.

ENDNOTE

1. In Hebraic understanding, this is a direct reference to Moses' ongoing virility.

CHAPTER TWO

HOT LINE TO HEAVEN

I learned some bedrock insight that I'll never forget from an anonymous quote recorded by Dr. Michael Brown in one of his books that gives us an unmistakably clear picture of just how corrupted an initially sacred design can become.

In the first century A.D. when our no-nonsense Galilee Rabbi challenged His people—along with their corrupt leadership in Jerusalem—to return to their God, what had originally been a massive popular movement of repentance, eventually "became a philosophy in Greece, an institution in Rome, a culture in Europe and an enterprise in America."[1]

It couldn't be said with more clarity; a self-seeking, self-worshipping, ingrown distortion of do-it-yourself legalism short-circuited the Divine Designer's blueprint of redemption to petty political power wrangling. And it has hardly happened just once over the last 2,000 years!

But let's expand on those devious detours from Heaven's highways even a bit more, and back to a much, much earlier point in time. Way back in the days of Noah, the moral integrity of the Creator's human family had fallen deeply into disarray. *"The Lord saw...that every inclination of the thoughts of* [man's] *heart was only evil all the time"* (Gen. 6:5), and a disappointed Architect of time and space designed a deluge of liquid judgment that washed away a corrupt and idolatrous society. Their earliest ancestors, having been evicted from that glorious garden of paradise potential, the only momentum for flow-on generations had been sadly downhill.

Noah surfaced from the morass, and the Almighty enjoined his righteous legacy to go for a second lap in the human race. That didn't last long either.

Babylon thereafter picked up the limelight as the demonic capital of the world, and when it comes to godlessness, idolatry, and such fruitless futilities, it only got worse. Finally, Nimrod ben Cush—a bit of a Mafia type—came along and got into "urban development" from Babylon to Nineveh to everywhere else in those parts, including an area called Shinar. That was the place that Nimrod and his gang got really enthused in skyscraper design that ended up not unlike Ground Zero in New York; except when his Babel tower fell flat, no one got killed—just scattered to the ends of the earth. (See Genesis chapters 10 and 11.) Moreover, the demons got more and more comfortable in those haunts. (The British invaded the area in 1921 and began calling it Iraq.) And it would seem that satan's little helpers are still operating around there with a reasonably relaxed impunity.

But then it starts to get better. The Almighty moved in earnest about improving not only the lot, but also the overall performance of His creation, and began a personal relationship with this more than resolute senior citizen we now know as Abraham. The first thing He wanted Abraham to do was to clear out of Babylon and environs because it was obviously not the most morally or spiritually inspiring neighborhood to live in. Thus, the Most High assigned him not only to begin that famous Hebraic family of redemption, but also to move on so that his later offspring could eventually found a corresponding city of polarity *against* demonic Babylon.

That city, of course, turns out to be Jerusalem. It has also come to be known by a number of other names like Mount Zion, Mount Moriah, or even the City of the Great King. But the description that paints the clearest name-picture of all is found some 20 times in the

Book of Deuteronomy alone when God speaks of His selected site to Moses as *"the place the Lord your God will choose as a dwelling for His Name"* (Deuteronomy 12:11; along with multiplied similar references throughout the Hebrew Scriptures). That interesting bit of divine choice just might have some bearing on the white-hot controversy that this bit of real estate yet generates in our day. The ghosts of Babylon's birthright are not all that impressed in having a Hebraic Jerusalem as a rival, and are endeavoring to de-Zionize the Creator's choice, claiming it as their own Islamic conquest.

Though this ongoing, if not escalating, violent disagreement is not totally central to the Hebraic trail we shall be tracing in the following chapters, it is an extremely significant segment of the heated issues within our current end-of-days scenario. And that makes it well worth understanding. I have covered a good deal of this in my earlier book, *Where Is the Body?*[2] which should be of value for additional background information.

But what we need to primarily turn our attention to here is that the God of the universe—who is scorned, scoffed at, and essentially written off by the masses—starts up this personal friendship with Abraham. They communicate. They talk together. Abraham is more than aware that he is being talked to, and he answers back. He asks questions. And he gets answers as well. These metaphysical ideas— that is, the supernatural—are not exactly mainstream in our secular-programmed 21st century, but that's the whole point. This God of Abraham is decidedly different.[3]

Never mind that many fancy folks think that this is a bit far-out—weird in fact. They just won't buy it—at least not these days, and that includes many whom society would classify as "religious." But in the next few chapters we're going to peek into a few heads throughout the ages as to *why* this is so, since it has had a reasonably impressive track record in *all* ages past. We'll play "psychological plumber" and check up on a few historical leaks of ye-old gray matter from a few of our famous forerunners who should have certainly known better!

Because you know what? A meaningful personal intimacy with our Maker works! In fact, it's standard fare for a lot of good people I know. We ask Him questions, and we get answers. There are times when we may have to wait a while, but it's worth it. We take our orders, and hopefully we have sense enough to carry them out.

Is this some new sect? No way! Basically, it's just quality prayer. But sad to say, to far too many petitioners, prayer is nothing more than a memorized monologue. Look, if Abraham had two-way communication with the Almighty, why can't I? And I can. No, I've never heard an audible voice. Those who hear "voices" usually have a problem or two! Though, seriously, I do know a few very credible folks of sound mind and sanity who have heard Him outright. But that's the problem with the *rigor mortis* of organized religion these days. What the secular society regards as "religion" never has redeemed anyone, but a relationship with the King of the Universe certainly does.

But again, what I may or may not happen to experience is not what this wake-up call is all about. It's just a bit of my own reinforcement of what I'm going to say next.

Abraham established a credible communication with his Creator that is a brilliant step forward—or should we say upward—for a created one to take. Questions like, "Does the clay say to the potter, 'What are you making?'" (Isa. 45:9) or, "Shall I hide from Abraham what I am about to do?"(Gen. 18:17-33) suggest both agreement and disagreement and reflect three things:

1) Communication with the Eternal *is normal.*

2) Communication with the Eternal *is practical.*

3) Communication with the Eternal *is a very valuable connection to cultivate.*

But this is hardly limited to an aging Abraham or a phenomenon with a few God-fearing, far-outs then or now. It's normative for anyone who wants to pursue quality life over and above the cultural rat race. With that in mind, let me say that it is difficult for anyone who brushes aside the privilege to converse one-on-one with his Maker, to measure the actual depth of his professed linkage with the King of kings!

Abraham's grandson Jacob had some monumental encounters as well, not the least with a representative of the Most High one night in a physical form. In the most bizarre of potter and clay run-ins, they had an all-night wrestling match. By the breaking of dawn, it appeared to have turned out to be somewhat of a draw since Jacob hung in there all night and wouldn't let go of the stronger Holy One. But since the "clay" Jacob was the lesser in strength of the two contenders, and yet was able to hold out for the entire night, Jacob was ultimately awarded the victory because *"you have struggled with God and with men and have overcome"* (Gen. 32:22-32). And he was blessed for it; it was at that point that God changed his name to Israel. Reminds us of, *"What is man that You are mindful of him?"* (Ps. 8:4a). But He certainly is mindful, and that to the point of conversing with us.

There are a number of accounts throughout both the *Tanakh*—our Hebrew Scriptures—and the New Covenant Scriptures where there was a credible human contact with something—actually Someone—greater in divine status than the lesser dreams or visions encounters often known as angels. From the study of Genesis 14 through 19, Abraham had both invisible and visible conversations. Moses obviously encountered Someone more than a bush-fire on the backside of Midian (see Exod. 3:2-6). Joshua meaningfully communicated with an ominous military Commander who was far more real than dream-dust just before the march on Jericho (see Josh. 5:13-15).

Then there are some eight mentions of the "angel of the LORD"[4] in the Book of Judges that suggest it was angelic-like in form; but from examining the whole text, it was obviously Someone quite a bit higher. And finally, the fourth member in the fiery furnace with Daniel's friends, always has suggested the person of a pre-incarnate Messiah-type (see Dan. 3:25). Let's face it, the King of the Universe is able enough to impressively present Himself as any kind of pre-20th century supernatural "cell phone" He likes, and can and will call on whomever or whenever. And He seems to come equipped with a magnificent storage system of any and all personal phone numbers! All of this makes any similar New Covenant supernatural encounters nothing really new with respect to all these recorded run-ins of Old Covenant precedent.

So the entire summary of this discussion is that the Hebraic culture under the God of the universe established a bona fide hot line with the Most High of Heaven that worked, and worked well—even astonishingly well at times for those who weren't even expecting a call! (See Numbers 22:21-35; 1 Samuel 3:1-18.)

But we will find in the next chapter there eventually arose a mind-bending battalion of brilliant strategists that prodded the world to presume that Abraham and Friend were nothing but phonies—preferably to be forgotten. And that, my friends, becomes the metaphysical or supernatural watershed of history. Let's hit the next page.

ENDNOTES

1. Michael Brown, *End of the American Gospel Enterprise* (Shippensburg, PA: Destiny Image Publishers, 1996), 75.

2. Victor Schlatter, *Where Is the Body?* (Shippensburg, PA: Destiny Image Publishers, 1999), Chapter 1, "A Man Called Abraham."

3. See the Hebraic view and benefits of this relationship in Deuteronomy 4:5-8.

4. Note that in this usage, English translations render /LORD/ with *all* capitals to signify the usage of the divine Name, whereas /Lord/ with only a beginning capital generally reflects merely a form of respect associated with "master" or "sir."

CHAPTER THREE

THE MIND-BENDERS TRY TO BEND BEDROCK

I find it fascinating to reflect on so much of the knowledge of the ancients that is still impacting us today. An insightful King Solomon proposed that, *"...there is nothing new under the sun"* (Eccles.1:9). Despite haughty Western world overconfidence in an age of unparalleled technology, we would do well to discover on the human edge that Solomon's words of wisdom were never more fitting than for our so-called "modern" world of egoism and insensitivity. It is an embarrassment that a "superior" minded West is so ignorant of what has happened before us, as well as those current happenings that could be tremendously valuable insights from other cultures and other lands.

An ironfisted Saddam Hussein of our own generation arose with a star-studded vision of valor in the Arab world by becoming a sort-of reincarnated protégé of Nebuchadnezzar. This notorious tyrant in the 1991 scourge of scud missiles upon Israel, happened to hail from the same general geography as his hero of 586 B.C., and thus Saddam had venerated him as some long lost kinsman.

And there were the Roman swords that dripped with blood giving ascendancy to Rome with the unrivaled power grip of the Caesars. Rome in turn left its supremacy stamp on a modern day

Europe that today vies for both economic and political power across the global map.

But the most long lasting of all such cultural-cum-political roots was scarcely from the blades of butchers. Rather it was the Greek Hellenist thought-merchants whose ideas globally surf-boarded in the beckoning watershed of the conquest of Alexander the Great. Planting enduring seeds into the minds of the masses who were keen to let others do their thinking for them, Greece's philosophers planted the roots of a world mind-set yet to come. The humanistic vision of One-World government and a New World Order is anything but new!

The Greek Hellenist thinkers appeared on the scene in what is sometimes suggested as the "silent years" of Scripture. They presented humanity with pleasant Greek-garlanded alternatives to a responsible human accountability to a higher authority. It was Socrates who began to present those less than Hebraic insights among his compatriots when he suggested that god was merely an impersonal presence of sorts that expressed himself in the beauty of his creations. Indeed, the God I know does that as well, and I do at times hear Him whispering as I walk in the gardens or woodlands, but I never quite saw eye to eye with the assumption that it might be merely the trees murmuring. We do seem to have a revival of tree-huggers among us these days, and my best post-Socratitic suggestion is that it is not the tree, but the Creator of the tree who has the greater compassion for understanding, not to mention an improved vocabulary for conversation!

In summary, by contrast with the earlier Hebraic discovery of a Creator God who cared and *responded*, Socrates and civilization's new Hellenist mentors replaced Him with a far less intrusive version of a more impersonal god, who it seems could not have cared less, and *absconded*. But if we truly have no Abba, how can we ever find our way in such an unfriendly, competitive, greedy, unprotected, dog-eat-dog environment? The Hellenistic answer is that if any of those presumed gods are so far off and disinterested, why not become our own god? And that, my friend, is called humanism, and we are there! Did I hear someone say, *"Take the fruit, Mrs. Adam's, and you'll be clever like God, knowing good and evil"*?

Anyway, Socrates and associates had room for all kinds of ideas about otherworldly gods, lucky stars, lucky charms, evil omens, and the like. Most were, however, brainy enough to know that carved or cast idols weren't all that valuable except for ending up in a glass case in a museum someday, and an idol-smashing Socrates reportedly demolished a few. (Had he been a bit sharper, he could have sold them for a few dinars to the Babylonians!) Unfortunately, Abraham and his Heaven-sent contacts came in last for creditability with these shrewd thinkers. Then at the ripe old age of 70, Socrates was nailed by his friends for "corrupting the youth" with his idol-bashing bent, and made him drink poison as his punishment. That didn't go down so well! And thus he died, leaving his prominent student Plato to carry on.

So enter Plato. Among all the other awe-inspiring ideas that Plato had, he did leave us with three credible clues of how humankind could increase their intelligence.

> The first was gaining knowledge through a teacher or by reading books (like this one)! Unfortunately, I haven't noted that Plato and his peers ever endorsed reading Moses or any other bits of the Hebrew Scriptures. Suffice it to say, his advice was to advance their insights by learning—preferably in Athens—with little or no mention of Hebrew University in Jerusalem! Without a doubt that was because they didn't get around to formally opening HU until 1925, which turned out a bit late for any Hellenistic kudos.

> Secondly, he taught that another mode of receiving information was through intuition. Most of the ladies are blessed with that. They can just "feel" when things are not quite right. In addition, my wife can find lost items like you wouldn't believe, though she recognizes that hers is a gift from Above. I don't recall if Plato would

have taken the time to suggest the *source* of intuition, but it will do to note that whatever his take on that may have been, he did list it as one other way the human mind can pick up valid data.

An interesting sideline in the reality of intuition, and the fact that it does come from a Higher Hand, is that it is observable as well in the animal world, where even the males seem to have their fair share. An excellent case in point was the devastation in the Indian Ocean environs by the tsunami of December 2004 when all the animals from rabbits to elephants seemed to have a built-in sense of the impending danger, and in advance of the event proceeded safely to higher ground.[1]

But it was Plato's third proposal of ways by which we may increase our knowledge of the world around us that created a significant rift with some of his colleagues. He termed it "Divine Madness,"[2] which included gaining information from the metaphysical or spirit world. Plato presumed that beyond good luck-bad luck concepts from chance happenings, insights from otherworldly sources such as the occult realm was possible as well. This, of course, might include séance-type messages from the world of darkness that was expressly forbidden in the Hebrew Scriptures (see 1 Sam. 28:1-14 for one of the better known examples). But on the other hand for God-honoring souls, this source of knowledge I would judge, must also include information from God Himself through His Holy Spirit, or I like the Hebrew—His *Ruach Ha Kodesh*.

So should Plato have adequately searched out the God of the Hebrews, he would have had to opt for this divine source as well. You can't have it both ways—if you're honest, that is.

We will probe the implications of Plato's thinking and its subsequent rejection by others in a later chapter. But suffice it to say at this point, that to the Hebraic point of view, Plato drew some very helpful conclusions with regard to the sourcing and interpretation of information.

But hold on, here comes the hassle! Aristotle, Plato's star pupil was not quite so convinced. Discounting any "Divine Madness" source of intelligence, Aristotle tossed out his mentor's concept of getting any meaningful insights from the supernatural realm. Good luck-bad luck from the impersonal stars? Possibly. Or fear-features from the less than likeable boogey-boys? Who knows? But secrets from outer space stayed right where they were. That was too far-out for Aristotle! And of course, along with anything else supernatural, that cut out any and all mentoring from the Most High of the Hebrews—not the least, that still small voice of the Holy Spirit.

But for any kind of knowledge formulated in the mind of man, it was "all systems go." Did I hear the word "humanism" out there in the audience?

And there we have it. Aristotle became the patron philosopher of the Western world's "sanitized wisdom." If you can't see it, it ain't there! And if *"...no one may see* [God] *and live"* (Exod. 33:20), then we shut our eyes and live without Him. And the Western world has most often unwittingly, yet invariably, done just that. We rationalize our phoniness into "enlightenment." We waltz with God with our words only, but in the realm of reality, the "religious" mind-set forever tries to cross that great dividing range of faith with Aristotelian uneasiness that it just might not be so. And the Western world is stuck with a god that moves nicely in theory, rhetoric, and brilliant programming, but dissolves like the morning dew when the nations ask, *"What happened to Abraham's God?"* (compare Ps. 79:10).

We'll pick up on the unfortunate damning influence of Aristotle again a bit down the line.

But before we leave the Hellenistic mindbenders on the back burner, one more philosopher, Pericles, dare not be overlooked. Pericles was pretty much the Papa of Democracy, as we know it. Now when it comes to corporately sharing one's ideas, feelings, and preferences, the concept of everyone having his say is actually not a bad thing. On the other hand, when it comes to actual practice and national allegiances, there are very few if any powerbrokers in global governments these days, from Saudi Arabia on up, that would take kindly to ceding one millimeter of governing priority to the One who said, *"My kingdom is not of this world"* (John 18:36a). It's okay if the Almighty keeps His place in some distant galaxy where He belongs, but we don't want to see any of His sovereignty ideas poking around into our halls of parliament or higher.

Nevertheless, the democratic concept of hearing from all concerned did start out as some reasonably helpful principles in those days. But as in any other historical system of human government, no dynasty—democratic or otherwise—has ever lasted much longer than 200 years before corruption, decay, totalitarian trends, and eventual overthrow set in. We should hardly expect what is called "democracy" today to fare any better. The Middle East, for example, yearns for "Western democracy" as much as I aspire—like some of the younger set—to dye my hair green.

Corrupted by massive wealth of the politicians, both before and after being "elected," as well as consolidation of a power base through graft and political horse-trading, the decadence of the political systems of the Western world have little to impress the have-nots of the Third World. Strategically a sovereign God has always used a nation more vile than the lip-service government that "should have known better" to bring down His wrath upon the guilty. In some sense, they knew it all along but took their chances. Obviously, even the terrorists think they are doing God—their own god—service.

In summary, the Greek Hellenists taught the Romans, and the Romans passed the ball to Europe, and Europe to the entirety of the Western world. And now these Hellenistic-seeded governments of our day are all converging into the global concept of a New World Order, arrogantly thinking—much as those religious institutions of yesteryear—that they *are* God. This is merely a secular rerun of the identical issue that calls for the separation of church and state, when a religious system became political, presuming it *is* God and speaks *for* God. The church learned it from Caesar, and Caesars then or now always yearn for a comeback!

But the One who said His Kingdom is not of this world did not mean that He wasn't going to be in charge one of these days. He merely informed Pilate that He wasn't a *politician* who would ever fit in with the Roman system—or any world government past or present for that matter.

For instance, Yeshua (that's Jesus, of course, but I like to use His Hebrew name) had *friends*. So does His Abba. By contrast, the following quote has been attributed to Lord Palmerston, Prime Minister of the United Kingdom back in the middle of the 19th century: "Nations have no permanent friends, just interests" confesses to quite another system. But that simple admission speaks for every Western government all the way up to the present. (Some have even omitted the word "permanent.") And for that matter, that political stance probably goes all the way back to Nimrod as well.

The moment of truth, therefore, is that there is no such thing as a "Christian" nation. Some of the Western world have come to realize this. Some have not. There are nations among the Gentiles that have a high percentage of Bible believers, including some of their leaders at times, but that hardly makes them "Christian." Governments get baptized with such things as tsunamis, floods, and hurricanes, but hardly with the "baptism of repentance"!

For those among us who may be a bit confused, the entire Western world today has an Aristotelian-cum-Periclean watershed of human government before us. There is one nation, and one nation only that has been forever marked out and set aside to never be like one of the nations (see Num. 23:9-10).

Unfortunately, the secular politicians of a primarily blinded Israel, hate that "chosen" bit with a passion and want to change that status so bad they can taste it. But that choice is hardly for a secular Israeli government. It's an irony, because the rest of the world from the United States to the United Nations to the European Union to the Arab League wants the baggage of a biblical Israel as much as the *whole world wants green hair!* But the Almighty is less than likely to change His mind! He has His own New World Order on the back burner, and serious-minded Bible believers are explicitly watching for that *"new heaven and a new earth"* (see Rev. 21:1-3).

So go and give it a bit of serious thought as to where your personal political allegiances happen to fall and why!

The bedrock of the Hebraic message of redemption has been subtly attacked but hardly replaced, has been shaken but hardly removed, has been ignored but hardly silenced. *"...Then they will know that I am the Lord"* occurs in Ezekiel 36:38 with a repeated declaration of that austere pronouncement occurring some 80 times throughout the entirety of the Hebrew Scriptures.

ENDNOTES

1. Could this phenomenon also have been a feature to assist Noah in his otherwise insurmountable task of a preservation of the species, throughout the period of the Great Flood?

2. Joseph Peiper, "Divine Madness": Plato's Case against Secular Humanism, http://www.amazon.com/exec/obidos/ASIN/0898705576/103-4484740-5517429.

CHAPTER FOUR

WHAT SADDENED THE SADDUCEES?

I N a monumental quotation by apostle Paul with regard to his passion to proclaim the death and resurrection of Yeshua, his newly discovered Messiah, he emphasized, *"to the Jew first..."* (compare Rom. 1:16). That head-of-the-line sequence sprang from his identity with an utmost concern for his own extended family and Jewish heritage. It's interesting that someone else also had similar sentiments to put the Jews at the top of their wish list, though for scarcely the same reasons—the Greeks!

Since the specialty of Hellenistic culture was propagating new and novel ideas, they were not a little impressed with their own panorama of the gods that they had lined up for veneration. But in contrast to traditional Middle East tribal thinking, where the sword and spear of conquerors dictated to the defeated what new gods they were now obliged to recognize, the culturally "superior" Greeks chose to invade the mind as well as the city shrine. After all, if you're so smart, why not try to prove it! And even though Aristotle had short-circuited any and all supernatural-generated information, this was hardly the only threat to the monotheism of Moses. Pagan practices and Hellenistic syncretism was always just around the corner, and because of their dogged determination, the Jews made a tantalizing target.

Led by Antiochus Epiphanes in 169 B.C. the Greeks had conquered Jerusalem, and in the vilest of anti-Semitic salt-in-the-wound, he desecrated the Temple sanctuary by sacrificing an abominable pig on the sacred altar. Five years later, against overwhelming military odds, Judas Maccabeus led a small band of the faithful to defeat the Hellenists and eventually cleanse and rededicate the Temple. Moreover, a less than cherished Antiochus died of unknown causes that same year. This glorious victory instituted the celebration of Hanukkah, the only Jewish feast not detailed for celebration in the Hebrew Scriptures, but given recognition in the New Covenant Scriptures. (See John 10:22.) Hanukkah was called Feast of Dedication in English, and it is evident from this text that Yeshua commemorated Hanukkah, as He would have all the sacred Feasts of Israel.

HEBRAIC RESOLVE VERSUS GREEK INFLUENCE, ROUND ONE:

For the Jews: Judas Maccabeus 1

For the Greeks: Aristotle 0

Unfortunately, the legendary game was not over.

Continuing to read on in the four Apocryphal books of the Maccabees—Hebraic lore and literature written between the Hebrew Scriptures and the New Covenant times—we learn more of the bold Maccabees in general and their hero, Judas "The Hammer" Maccabeus in particular. In later years it appears, unfortunately, that their descendants were something less than diligent by contrast with their forebears. Becoming diverted to the ever-enticing potential of personal pride (what else is new under Solomon's sun?), the latter offspring of the onetime Maccabee faithful, sadly found substitute fascination with Greek-flavored pomp, prestige, and political power.

And the name of their new game just happened to be Temple Politics. Looks like some additional Sanhedrin rededication cum housecleaning well might have been in order!

Then seemingly too close to call coincidence, a new sect of the Jews called the Sadducees surfaced right in this same general time-frame. Though few records have been found to nail down their exact origins, their appearance around 200 B.C. is suspiciously close to the above mentioned meltdown era of Maccabee morality. They had come to mainstream Temple prominence by the days of Yeshua, but were hardly heralded in the Scriptures for any kindly recognition they might have offered the King of the Jews! And they faded from glory—not to mention history—shortly after the destruction of the second Temple in A.D. 70. Historian, Josephus Flavius, mentions them in his writings, but other than religious politics as their standard bill of fare, not a great deal of other distinctive behavior is recorded.

Except for one grand give-away literary snapshot in the Book of Acts!

Paul, the apostle, had been hauled into the religious court for preaching the resurrection of Yeshua. Now this was pretty much one of his favorite subjects, even though it didn't gain him too many friends nor influence too many delegates in the Sanhedrin of the day. Fortunately, the good apostle had an impressive record of thinking on his feet; and he looks first to the right and then to the left, and he notes that the courtroom is full of both Pharisees and Sadducees. Now Paul was of Pharisee origins and kinship, and despite the fact that some of his clansmen didn't take too kindly to his message, he still retained a good bit of latent nostalgia to his Pharisee roots. He comes off with, "You Sadducees are just on my case because I'm a Pharisee and believe in the resurrection." Well that lit the fuse, and with the little argument that erupted between the Pharisees and the Sadducees, Court was all over for that day at least! But why? *"The Sadducees say that there is no resurrection, and that there are neither angels nor spirits, but the Pharisees acknowledge them all"* (Acts 23:8). The full story about Paul's court fiasco is found in Acts 23:6-10, and two other passing references to the Sadducees are found in Acts 4:2 and Mark 12:18.

There it is. So who were these Sadducees? Wherever they hailed from, they were religious Jews who had been heavily influenced by the Hellenists in general and Aristotle in particular, who—as we will well remember—threw out the Platonic concept of "Divine Madness" and molded the Western mind forever to a psychological prison cell purged of anything that smelled of the supernatural. Unfortunately, the Good Book sanitized from the spiritual is not a good book at all!

HEBRAIC RESOLVE VERSUS GREEK INFLUENCE BY THE END OF ROUND TWO:

For the Jews: Judas Maccabeus 1

For the Greeks: Sadducee Puppets 1

The Greeks tied it all up in the second half, and that's the tally that remains on the scoreboard to this very day. Half of world Jewry continues on in a path of secular Western bondage with the presumption that their Hebrew heritage had no spiritual life in it, while a God-fearing remnant yet remains who still call on the God of Abraham, Isaac, and Jacob—plus an ever increasing number who call on the Abba of Yeshua as well.

Okay, that's about Jews. But what about professed followers of the Eternal One in Gentile circles? Just because someone is the member of a Christian congregation, does this guarantee his relationship with, or comprehension of, the magnitude of His Creator—if he even believes in a Creator at all? Or what of those who have been "born again" out of a pit of misery, guilt, and frustration? So far so good, but have they then progressed far enough to explore the majesty of an intimate personal communication with the King of the Jews?

Having mulled that over, just how far off the wall does much of Christendom think that Aristotle actually was to jettison this "Divine Madness" thing anyway? Just how much phoniness does most of the Western world—Christianity included—tack on to the supernatural realm in our time? Unfortunately, the fun and games of Harry Potter, witches, horoscopes, and occult dabbling are fair entertainment, but it's the down-to-earth moral issues that involve the supernatural that are out—far out.

Let me share with you a bit of my own personal journey into the inner echelons of the spiritual "unseen." If there is such a thing as "baptism by fire," then the "baptism of the unknown" might be equally descriptive. I grew up with a moderate Bible-belt knowledge of all the Bible stories from Adam to Zacchaeus. The Bible told me there were demons and angels, cherubim, and a crafty creature named satan (no capital "s" thanks). I assumed they were real 2,000 years ago, but I never saw any of these metaphysical manifestations, nor did I ever expect to. Thanks to brainy old Aristotle, I had a typical Western split-cosmology. Just as one young kid in Sunday school defined faith: "Faith is believing what you know ain't so!"

Not a great deal changed over the years on my split-level mentality of the metaphysical.

I graduated from a Big-Ten university with a degree in science, and followed through for seven years with a major American blue-chip company on the front lines of nuclear energy.

But eventually I got a signal from the Most High. (Mind you, He always had been a bit more real than the shadier side in the Scriptures that dealt with His enemy.) I then burned the bridges I had built climbing the professional ladder in nuclear energy long before it became politically correct to do so, and returned to another university to study linguistic analysis and Bible translation with the Wycliffe Bible Translators. Our family ended up in the Highlands of wild and wooly Papua New Guinea to translate the Scriptures into the heretofore unanalyzed and unwritten Stone Age language of the Waola people—one of 800 languages in that linguistic paradise of the South Pacific.

No demons so far!

But I want to minimize my story here—it's published in other literature—except to say that our new Stone Age buddies were anything but dummies. We discovered that the Waola language had over 100 ending-options on every verb. When we entered the tribe in

1961, there happened to be a young infant in his mother's arms who today holds a degree in law from the University of Papua New Guinea. Moreover, he currently heads up a law firm in the capital, Port Moresby. Neither his grandfather nor even his father had ever worn a pair of pants!

Sadly, much of the Western world would have classified these folks as mentally undernourished because they didn't speak English, yet they never stumbled upon the simple clue that Westerners weren't all that sharp either, because neither could they communicate in Waola! (One other famous European culture comes to mind that might have also relegated my Waola friends to the bumble basket because they didn't know French!)

I often quip that I got my advanced degrees in the same University that Moses did—on the backside of the mountain! Our Waola family comprises some of the greatest people on earth, and we learned immeasurable volumes from them, from Stone Age insights to tribal etiquette to Third World morality. I tell you I would never be writing books of international distribution had I not had the privilege of being mentored from a worldview unscathed by Hellenistic hiccups!

But then those supernatural studies!

I'll never forget hearing a young pastor mutter something about "feeling" a demon leave an unfortunate who was unquestionably possessed. He was totally out of it. Nor will I ever forget the *day and the hour* when—most unprepared and unsuspecting—I encountered the same phenomenon, something like a few microseconds of low-voltage electric shocks across my entire body. Except interestingly enough, it occurred in a benign Western home setting some 5,000 kilometers away from the enchanted Papua New Guinea Highlands! And being born as a Westerner with the "baptism of Aristotle," as well as steeped in scientific analysis, I am hardly one to be a victim of psychosomatic suggestion.

Identifying supernatural callers by now is old hat. In our Papua New Guinea circumstances I hardly relegated these uninvited visitors to the fear-file, but perhaps more realistically slotted them into a sort of "pesky" folder. Most turned out to be more of a nuisance like flies and mosquitoes—and just as vulnerable, I might say, to getting zapped. And you know what? Once my eons-before buddies found that I wouldn't laugh at them in crass Western fashion, I got a database on the supernatural like you wouldn't believe. Sorry, Aristotle, but you blew your chance to pick up some real clues from Stone Age University where they give un-ledgered doctorates in demonology!

The good news is that these encounters are hardly routine fare, but they do happen and they are as genuine as the common cold.

But most certainly, I would warn any and all that to inordinately focus on the spirit realm is a bit of a tightrope tango between idolatry and occult mentality. On the other hand, to deny the existence of the metaphysical cosmos is to reduce the enormity of the God of the galaxies to the mere size of a pastor, priest, or rabbi. But that analogy *exactly* captures the monumental wool that a less than credible Aristotle has drawn over the fleecy worldview of the Western world.

The Sadducees are our first and prime examples of metaphysical myopia (read: supernatural shortsightedness) in a people who otherwise profess to promote God. While on the Gentile side of the street, society has shaved God down to the size of a bishop, and the whole world either sleeps in or goes fishing.

Now let's move to the next chapter to see just how mischievously Aristotelian doctrine messed up even more of the church than we have uncovered thus far.

CHAPTER FIVE

FATE OF OUR FATHERS LIMPING STILL

W E will certainly *not* be featuring in this chapter the pious papas who perished in the flames of France or the arenas of Rome. Instead, there were those other less than faithful fathers of the faith who disappointingly had become over-impressed with the insights of Aristotle, and their flocks suffered the slow death of secularization. Needless to say, the legacies that most of these left behind were something much less than helpful.

Moreover, still others among those church fathers had also degenerated into dyed-in-the-wool anti-Semites whose corresponding doctrines had likewise slowly descended into a diet of hate. Limping, yes, because as is sometimes the case, many of their followers diligently pressed on, miraculously bypassing the decadence of their leaders, so all was not lost. Abba was looking on from a distance, and today, many of their followers still knit to the Scriptures, persistently plod on with a message of hope.[1] But yes, some do still unfortunately limp, because there was a serious injury or two from days gone by that has never healed to this day. And sad to say, that dragging of the feet continues to reflect that all is still not well.

If the Sadducees and associates got hung up on Olympic-like political arm wrestling within the Sanhedrin, what's wrong with a bit of good old ecclesiastical horse-trading in the fledgling church? Of course, those Dark Age debacles would hardly happen anymore these days among the myriad of dog-eat-dog sectarian stances that surfaced after the Reformation. Better reflect a bit on that one as well!

Moreover, if we pretend to not notice and want to look the other way, we may well bump into the same phantom that also seduced the Sadducees. Bad theology on supernatural authority bedeviled the European church from then to now in misjudging the metaphysical by presuming it either didn't exist or else that it had been replaced by humans who were too god-like to question.

Another track would have been the presumption that evil as such had no definable dark side that might require subduing, yet all the while naively thanking their lucky stars that "fate" happened to be on their side now and again. How can we get it so turned upside down? Yet, C.S. Lewis reminded us that "demons are not made from bad fleas or bad mice, but from bad archangels."[2]

But worst of all, while religiously presuming the theory that there was a Spirit of God that brooded over the waters in creation, those admirers of Aristotle never had a clue that He would in reality engage the individual believer in vital communication with the King of the Universe, much less fill him with power as an anointed representative of the Most High. No demons, no angels, no real assurance of a resurrection, no moral victory, no spiritual power— no difference than the Hellenists!

Thus, just as the Sadducees and secular Jews who followed them fumbled with the power switch—no less did the Gentile church that bumbled along into that same Aristotelian blindness that short-circuited any personal involvement with a supernatural universe. Hardly a surprise, those "enlightened" ones eventually concluded that a spirit world may not even exist at all.

But here's one more interesting if not vital bit of history to secure the link:

Guess who eventually latched on to Aristotle as his favorite guru of philosophical influence? No less than St. Thomas Aquinas, the 13th-century doctor cum theologian, lecturer in church doctrine,

and leading intellectual of the day. He was especially noted for fus-
ing theology with philosophy—brilliant thinking to some but crass
Christo-paganism to others. Aquinas reckoned that his Hellenist
hero who had demoted Plato's "Divine Madness" deductions to
moon-dust, was about the greatest mentor since Moses, and most
probably even preferred him to that Jewish born has-been.

And quite in parallel with the Sadducees, that has had an amazing amount to do with why the average Western churchman to this
very day limits his liaison with the supernatural in general—and the
Holy Spirit in particular—to little more than lip service. Go figure!

And then there's this celibacy thing. A meteoric rise in the number of lawsuits of late, attests to the fact that celibacy as a mandat-
ed program has a few problems. God didn't put us together that
way. In no way do I even suggest passing judgment on any God-
fearing soul who commits himself or herself to a life of chastity as
a personal commitment for whatever reason. It can and does work.
But in the norm, the Designer of Life had other ideas. Hebraically,
this is more than recognized as we noted in Chapter One in the
Garden blessings. Moreover, there is a rabbinic blessing, not to mention biblical, for every thing in physical life, including bodily func-
tions from the more mundane—food in, food out—to the more
magnificent aspects of procreation as extolled in Psalm 139:13-14;
Proverbs 5:18-19; Ephesians 5:28-32; and by all means, the entire
allegory of the Song of Songs. While even on the practical level, the
first thing the surgeon wants to know after abdominal surgery is if
the divine plumbing still works! And when it does, there is great
rejoicing with follow-on thanksgiving to Heaven if the patient happens to be a God-fearing believer.

But look, that's not really my main focus. This issue merits neither my personal judgment nor my benevolent blessing; what my
brother does in this case is none of my business. But our very significant point here is how did church leadership happen to get from
a Hebraically rabbinic lifestyle of procreation to the exact opposite—celibacy for the leadership? I do have a problem of tagging it
on to the Holy Spirit.

With all honesty of research, it's just one more example of Hellenistic-inspired divergence from the Creator's Plan A. The Stoics kicked the football to the Romans who passed it on to the church who grabbed it and ran. Sadly, in recent days too many players have been dropping the ball!

So who were these Stoics anyway?

Stoicism was one additional "enlightened" Greek philosophy whose highest goal was impassive indifference to pleasure or pain. Putting aside passion, inordinate thoughts, or indulgence notched them a cut above those who muddled with the mundane matters of physical procreation. Blend this with those elite intellectuals in the Hellenist society who prided themselves with more lofty ideas than cavorting around the gymnasiums in their birthday suits, and you had a ready-made two-tiered society—those who orbited with the elite and those who got their feet muddy. Not exactly linked to obedience versus disobedience of Mosaic standards, but two-tiered nevertheless!

Then we move on to observe the Romans around second century B.C.,and we find that Stoicism and its trimmings caught on with Rome a bit better than any other of the preceding Greek mindgames. Regrettably, the church faithful picked up on a misguided spiritual potential of a two-level society, and there you have it. In the beginning it was not so! More Hellenist hand-me-downs that the West could have done without!

Then there are Greek-loaded semantics of how the church fathers began to view the King of the Universe. If there is anything that sets the God of Abraham apart from any and all of His deity-delving predecessors (not to forget any and all of those who followed after), it was *monotheism*. The bedrock text of the Jews that echoed from Sinai was, *"Hear O Israel: The Lord our God, the Lord is one..."* (Deut. 6:4). That and the next five verses are written on a tiny scroll and inserted into a small ornate box called a mezuzah in specific compliance with Deuteronomy 6:9. They can be seen fastened on not a few million doorposts (including interior doors) in Israel, not to mention some millions more in God-fearing Jewish homes in the Diaspora.

Seems like it holds a tad of importance to the Jews—not the ornate box but the message within—one God and one only!

Now all Gentile believers are more than prompt to agree to the Ancient of Day's singular identity, but thanks to our Hellenist new-idea peddlers, they believe one thing but suggest quite the opposite in the oft presented "God the Father, God the Son, and God the Holy Spirit" sequence. When stated in that succession, it doesn't demand a Master's Degree in Math to count 1-2-3 Gods, in that order, and it drives our God-seeking, God-honoring Jewish friends wild—and well it should. There's a far less confusing, far more accurate, and even far more biblical way to say it.

There is one God only—King of the Universe. His breath is the Holy Spirit—*Ruach Ha Kodesh* in Hebrew—that literally means "Holy Breath." Moreover in His declaration of atonement and seal of redemption, a *Ruach*-filled, Abba-related but human-born Yeshua, represents His right arm of salvation. *"Surely the arm of the Lord is not too short to save,"* which metaphor is reiterated in a multiplicity of Scriptures, the majority of which specify *"His **right** arm,"* a very Hebraic connotation of status.[3] This is indelibly consistent with the Almighty's promise to Moses that, *"I will raise up for them a prophet like you from among their brothers; I will put My words in his mouth, and he will tell them everything I command him"* (Deut. 18:17-18).

And that Hebraic concept speaks of *one God only* whose breath not only communicates His guidance to His people, but the corresponding power to carry it out. And Yeshua, His Abba's *right arm* of authority, is *not* another God but an integral part of God Himself, demonstrating His mercy, justice, and righteousness, as well as that long-promised redemption.[4]

And where does Yeshua happen to be positioned today? At the right hand of the Father! (Col. 3:1). There is one and only one God of Abraham, Isaac, and Jacob. His dimensions are incomprehensible; His breath is His Spirit of power; and His right arm is His means of redemption. Sounds like one God to me, and the Son is nonetheless for it.

That's straightforward enough to any simple Bible believer, but it took the Greek wise guys, whose pagan polytheism never seemed much of a problem to them, to succeed in putting a massive hatchet between God-fearing Jews and Bible-believing Gentiles for 2,000 years with their less than scriptural-styled semantics.

And these Hellenistic innovations in turn led to two millennia of vitriolic anti-Semitism that erupted into a mountain of distrust, misinformation, ghettos, persecution, pogroms, violent hatred, bloodshed, and finally the Holocaust. Don't try to tell me it didn't come from pagan Greco-Roman influence into the primitive and medieval-minded church. Here are the factual records from Wikipedia:

EARLY CHRISTIAN STATES' POLICIES WITH REGARDS TO JEWS AND NAZI GERMANY

There were Nazi policies toward Jews based or similar to state laws enacted in Europe by Christian rulers centuries before Nazism. The following are examples that were similar to Nazi policy.

- The Synod of Clermont (Franks), 535 C.E.[5], prohibited Jews from holding public office.

- Nazi Germany, 1935 C.E. — Prohibited Jews from holding public office.

- The 12th Synod of Toledo (Spain), 681 C.E., ordered the burning of the Talmud and other Jewish books.

- Nazi Germany — Ordered the burning of the Talmud and other Jewish books.

- In 692, the Trulanic Synod forbade Christians to go to Jewish doctors, attend Jewish religious feasts, or have friendly relations with Jews.

- Nazi Germany — The Nuremberg laws forbade people to go to Jewish doctors.

- The Fourth Lateran Council, 1215 C.E., forced Jews to wear a distinctive badge on their clothing.

- Pope Paul IV, in 1555, issued a papal bull forcing Jews to wear yellow hats; this same papal bull confined Jews to ghettos, and banned them from working in most professions.

- Nazi Germany adopted every one of these laws in 1939; the only change was that the yellow hat was changed to a yellow star.

- In the 1930s Nazi Germany helped the Lutheran church and other Christian churches publicise Martin Luther's teachings; his recommendations were carried out on every Jew in Germany and its occupied lands.[6]

It is certainly true that from the earliest days of the church there were bouts of distrust bouncing back and forth in both directions between Yeshua-believing Jews and Gentiles and their mainline counterparts in Judaism. Many Judaic leaders either mistrusted or misunderstood Paul's encounter with Yeshua. But by the same token in the opposite direction, Italian born St. Ignatius of Antioch took a strong stand against Gentile believers as early as A.D. 107, who wanted to keep the Sabbath in identity with, and the convictions of, their adoptive Jewish family at large. Again, it was the church fathers who rejected the Hebraic roots.

But the bombshell occurred—not an unfamiliar metaphor these days for Israel's friends and neighbors—when Emperor Constantine entered the flock, consolidated it under Rome's authority, and basically took over with a more than latent pagan Roman mentality. He pulled the plug on any and all Jewish heritage and relationships that the believers in Yeshua had with their former friends and family, not to overlook their bedrock heritage of the Hebrew foundations of Torah and the Tanakh.[7] He substituted pagan holidays for biblical ones, fertility symbols for Passover freedom, and replaced the Jewish-tainted Maccabean celebration of God's miracle of Hanukkah, by proposing instead a birthday party for Jesus—now no longer a despised Jew, but "one of us!"[8]

God forbid that we ever knock anyone for honoring the King of the Jews on December 25 in an effort to bless God. I say take every opportunity in season and out.

But I must also say that Constantine and not a few of his faithful followers must annually end up with a bit of egg on their faces around that time of the year. Why? It's Hebraic to celebrate a joyous birth—including angelic choirs on occasion—but *never* a birthday. The Good Book says, *"The day of death* [is] *better than the day of birth"* (Eccles. 7:1b). That's because when the blessed bundle is born, it's a majestic day for Mom and Dad, but the little fellow himself has never yet lifted a finger to the confrontations of life! But by the time he passes back to his Abba in Heaven, he has a bit of a bio to bring in hand.

True, Yeshua had His bio before He ever separated from the celestial realm, but why might He be less than impressed with a Birthday Party? Because the only two birthday celebrations recorded in the Good Book are Pharaoh's and Herod's. Both of these notorious tyrants were involved in not a little gruesome bloodletting. One would think that Yeshua would not be overly honored to make it into a trio, not to mention sharing the stage with Santa Claus (see Gen. 40:18-23; Matt. 14:6-12). But thanks anyway for trying to be thoughtful, Con.

We must here hark back to one memorable quote from *Where Is the Body?* "The church unwittingly sat down on the Emperor Constantine's pet porcupine and unfortunately we're still pulling out the quills today!"[9]

So much for Greco-Roman pagan influence on a fledgling church!

ENDNOTES

1. See "Church in the Wilderness," an interesting study that documents that even in the darkest days of spiritual decadence, there was always a Bible-oriented stream of the faithful that maintained a more biblically-oriented position.. http://www.biblesabbath.com/wilkerson/tttoc.htm

2. C.S. Lewis, *The Screwtape Letters* (New York, NY: Macmillan Publishing Company, Inc.,1973).

3. The Scriptures contain a myriad of texts denoting God's Arm/Right Arm of salvation or redemption including Isa. 48:13; 50:2; 59:1; Num. 11:23; Ps. 16:8; 80:17; 110:1,5; Mark 16:19; Col. 3:1; Heb. 1:13; 12:2; to list a few.

4. See also an impromptu personal encounter in Victor Schlatter, *Where Is the Body?* (Shippensburg, PA: Destiny Image Publishers, 1999), 16-17.

5. "C.E." refers to Common Era or Christian Era, an alternate rendering of the Latin, A.D. or *Anno Domini.*

6. See: Christianity and anti-Semitism from www.answers.com: http://www.answers.com/topic/christianity-and-anti-semitism?hl = nazi&hl = nuremberg&hl = laws. Scroll down to: "Comparisons between Nazi Germany and early Christian states' policies with regards to Jews."

7. The Torah and Tanakh comprise the Hebrew Scriptures that the church refers to as the Old Testament. The Torah is the initial five books of Moses; and the Tanakh is an acronym that includes the Torah, the Prophets, and the Writings, which include the Psalms and poetic books plus the remaining books of Hebrew history.

8. Victor Schlatter, *Where Is the Body?* (Shippensburg, PA: Destiny Image Publishers, 1999), Chapter 6, "The Paganization of Christianity."

9. Ibid., 53.

CHAPTER SIX

THE "MATCHLESS" AGE OF ENLIGHTENMENT

O KAY. We've just limped through those Dark Ages—say from the 5th to around the 15th century—and noted that the world by then was more than ready for a bit more light. But you know why the Dark Ages were so dark? There was witchcraft, Bubonic Plague—Black Death they called it—superstition, gross injustice, persecution of the poverty stricken, and last but hardly least, anti-Semitism. Lord Acton said it well: "Power corrupts and absolute power corrupts absolutely."[1]

And that which called itself the church in those days had the power. Not even the Most High dared interfere, not that He would have wanted to identify with some of the corruption! It was the darkest spiritual morass that the Gentile believers in the God of Abraham ever knew—and for sure not a good time to be one of the "chosen people" either! Whatever happened to that city set on a hill whose light could not be hidden? Or the Light of the World—where had He gone?

But you know what really made it such a miserable backwater era? Look, I never personally received this as divine revelation, but there ought to be a few clues that we should be picking up directly from the unmistakable message of the Good Book. Remember when the Almighty told Abraham that, *"I will bless those who bless you, and whoever curses you I will curse...."*? (Gen. 12:3). God repeats that again through Isaac to Jacob; and then again Isaac jogs Esau's memory with this moment of truth after he blew his birthright bonus for a bowl of beans. And the Almighty's special concern for the preservation of Israel and for protection of the *"apple of His eye"* is alluded to enough times throughout the Scriptures to demand our undivided attention on the matter. (See Zechariah 2:7-9 and Deuteronomy 32:9-10.)

And that's one sure prophecy that has been borne out over and over and over again. The world, as a whole, has never treated the Sons of Jacob all that well, but if any lengthy period in history was bleakest for the Jew, the Dark Ages were it. Because of their diet and sanitation habits as prescribed by Moses in the *Torah*, they encountered far fewer effects than did their Christian neighbors from the Bubonic Plague that swept Europe in the middle of the 14th century. Thus, rumor even had it that the Jews were behind this evil pestilence by "poisoning the Gentile wells," heaping all the more unwarranted heaviness on the hated Jew.

They were later herded into ghettos, restricted in their choice of occupation, maimed and murdered, and repeatedly run out of town. Sadly, this did not all end at the close of the Middle Ages, which was another way of designating the latter half of the Dark Ages.

And dark they were. The world writhed in need of a bit more light—much more!

Then it finally happened—that "matchless" Age of Enlightenment. I'll find a candle if someone has the matches! That quip poses the burning question: Just how light was the enlightenment?

For technical achievement there is no doubt whatsoever of the birth of great minds. Today from those rudimentary roots we have everything from instant global communication in cyberspace to snooping into heretofore hidden galaxies millions of light-years away. And humankind has even visited some of our nearer celestial neighbors either in person or by hi-tech proxy. May we even mention those noxious little nuclear devices that will wipe an entire city off the map with one order from the top, and a simple press on the button some distance down the chain of command!

Thus, when it comes to morals, ethics, and all-inclusive spiritual dimensions, it looks like we're going to need my candle, your matches, and more!

Just to give an example, in a mere 300-year tenure of development, we now have mega-politics that give us mega-freedoms—well, at least the elite do what they please—that furnish us with mega-superpower states that give the fortunate few a standard of living that was beyond mega-comprehension back in those dark, dark days of feudalism, 100-year wars, and accompanying bloodletting.

Okay, so less than 20 percent of the world's some 6 billion economic "battlers" are actually well enough off to survive with sufficiency and die with dignity, but we're working on those other unfortunate 80 percent. Never mind that the landslide to global poverty is a bit stubborn, and—quite out of character for a democratically conceived landslide—is heading downhill fast!

So how did we ever get into this economic pit of global poverty after such a marvelous era of enlightened discoveries? After opening the hideous Pandora's box of gas warfare in World War I—not to mention those 6 million Jews who perished by the same fate in World War II—Thomas Hardy penned: "After 2,000 years of [Christian] Mass, we've got as far as poison gas."[2]

Yet others were far more fascinated by the "freedom" options that loomed large for future generations, giving an alternate description for the period 1600-1800 as the Age of Reason. Both Jean Paul Sartre and Thomas Paine wrote books about this illuminating breakthrough of intelligence, somewhat surprisingly using the same title, *The Age of Reason*. These were the days when they began prescribing personal freedoms and human rights (what else is new?), and at one point Paine wrote that he "detested the Bible and detested everything else that was cruel," which opinion I would suggest ranked him a bit less Hebraic than even our buddy Aristotle. Anyway, after a bit of a stint in a French jail for writing the wrong things, Paine published another pamphlet in 1795 called

Common Sense. Ironically, that didn't change his poverty status all that much, and he died in America an outcast and penniless in 1802.[3]

Indeed, in that era there were all kinds of valuable scientific discoveries—chemistry, astronomy, medicine, optics, physics, biology, and a host more. But most of those initial scientists started out on a vastly different wavelength than those presumed to be the "great thinkers" of the Age, as well as some of the later scientists of laboratory levels.

Sir Isaac Newton (1642-1727) was dubbed "the Father of Science" while to others, René Descartes (1569-1650), who had appeared one century earlier, was awarded a similar title by those who had recognized his efforts, namely "the Father of Modern Science and Philosophy." But get this: Both men were devout believers in Abraham's best Friend, and both had a strong affinity to the Hebrew Scriptures. It was said of Newton, "Though he is better known for his scientific achievements, the Bible was Sir Isaac Newton's greatest passion. He devoted more time to the study of Scripture than to science and said, 'I have a fundamental belief in the Bible as the Word of God, written by those who were inspired. I study the Bible daily.'"[4]

Less comment is made about Descartes' affinity to Scripture, but philosophically he maintained that God was the only connection between the mind and the physical world. He viewed, "the physical world as mechanistic and entirely divorced from the mind, the only connection between the two being by intervention of God."[5]

Copernicus (1473-1543), the renowned discoverer of the heliocentric nature of our galaxy, held a high regard for Scripture as well. His protégé Galileo (1564-1642), who gave us the telescope, also had time for interpretation of the Holy Writ and interestingly enough, had a strong disdain for our friend Aristotle's views on astronomy!

Other high-profile, early contributors in the sciences were Johannes Kepler (1571-1630), the mathematician-astronomer, and Robert Boyle (1627-1691), the early chemist, who discovered Boyles Law (which I recall all too well from my undergraduate years in

Chemistry). Both were profound believers in the God of creation and more than recognized His involvement in their insights and achievements.[6]

Now this all interests me to the utmost because of my initial education in science, chemistry, and mathematics, with an eventual seven-year tenure in industrial post-graduate nuclear energy. Thus I too have had, and still maintain, a depth in the scientific method with a definite identity with where these early notables were coming from.

So here's my point. There's not one, but two ways to study science. There are Aristotle's insights of the abstract, or by stark contrast there are Solomon's sources of wisdom. Let's have a look at both:

> "Intelligent Design," that is, an Infinite Intelligence had to be behind it all. *"In the beginning God..."* (Gen. 1:1). Someone did it, so how did He do it? The Scientific Method obediently puts the pieces together.

> Or alternately—from infinite cosmos to a unique status called life—it all began somehow, somewhere, as an event something between coincidence and accident! The Scientific-Alternative Search therefore presumes we start guessing somewhere in the middle without the aid of any supernatural insights or foundation whatsoever. The last thing we would want to acknowledge is an Abba of accountability!

Now that kind of approach can't happen right away, because obviously Cosmic Roulette takes time. When you don't even have stuff like hydrogen, nitrogen, and oxygen to play Lunar Lego's, there's nothing to do but wait. At first, there's *nothing* to analyze, not even for those other scientists who had *not* been intimidated by the concept of a Creator. Then whammo, and there is *something*. And to fudge a bit further on the fantasy, some billions of years later my mega-great, great grandfather does the backstroke out of some swamp slime. Now if that's brilliance, then their god is a firecracker. That's probably so, because he's truly blown it and is no longer in business. Something is sick here. Is there a Hellenist in the house?

How on earth did we ever get back into this deep, dark hole after so much "enlightenment"?

I'll tell you how. Not only did we have the "enlightened" non-god scientists suggesting the alternative origins of the physical in those days, but we also had a spate of how-can-you-know philosophical "mind-mechanics" to probe the probabilities of matters that can't be proven.

Moreover, an astounding number of these philosophers favored *Aristotle's left-turn assumptions* that the metaphysical—if not merely made up in the mind—was totally impersonal and hardly inclined to give out cosmic clues to earthlings. So in good Hellenist fashion, a Creator was out, humanism was in, and those who spoke for an age of "enlightenment" were more impressed with what *humans* happened to think, than to be humbled by any condescending cues from Above.

What is more, in recent times these self-styled spokesmen have run into a gold mine of massive support. A voice-of-the-gods global media has offered their generous aid to crush the idiocy of any hint of Divine authority over their unabashed agenda to deify the god of human hands!

These modern manufacturers of truth belt out anti-God messages from Creator-less nature or discovery series, talk shows, sit-coms, soapies, movies, and videos to even politically correct interpretation of (read: propagandized) newscasts. The late Peter Jennings admitted it without apology: "There is no truth, only news."[7] Neither is there any longer a Voice in the heavens above nor on the earth beneath that can counter that Aristotelian shaped mind-set for a most high media! The minds of mankind must be sanitized from any Supreme Authority that would dare pose a challenge to a New World Order—and above all, anything with Hebraic roots!

Did I hear another echo of that earliest legless lizard giving his how-to-be-like-God advice? "Mrs. Adam's, I just ran into the coolest recipe on god-turnovers. You just add one slice of fruit from that unique looking tree over there on Center Circle!"

Regrettably, most of the early theologians from the fourth century onwards minored in philosophy—or had it become their major? From evaluation of the annals of time, it appears that this profession was far more likely to be influenced by our Hellenistic heroes than their counterparts who merely measured molecules, probed the planets, or calculated their courses. Note this: It appears that those who strove to study the galaxies had a far higher probability of seeing the shadow of the Almighty out there somewhere than those who peered introspectively into the human head.

Does that suggest to you any hindsight into the stepping-stones of Aristotle's conclusions to where we find ourselves today?

Finally, as we wind up this search into the seeming seduction of true science, out of the misty past a shadowy sight seems to remind us of the 19th-century rerun of the original Garden of not-to-be Eaten. And in the very center of the Garden we can just make out that now familiar tree of the *Perception of Light and Darkness*. And over at the side appears to be the most controversial of all the prominent Age of Enlightenment performers, Charles Darwin— 1809-1882.

To be or not to be—to be light or to be darkness—that is the question!

Without a shade of doubt there is an enormous amount of truth in Darwin's discoveries in genetic mutation and the evolvement of vast variations in the species due to environmental and climatic forces. But the bombshell—and there were even bigger bangs to follow—was that Darwin had crossed a red line of then-ethical scholarship.

In broad educational circles, a totally God-oriented identity with any or all issues would hardly be expected; nevertheless honest academic research does warrant evenhandedness. Whether by association or even from the overt applause from an atheistic cheering section of those days, we must note Darwin's lasting influence upon the watershed of Hebraic light versus Hellenistic darkness. Towering above and beyond any of his valued scientific insights, was his dubious philosophical detour in craftily pulling the rug of reality out from under mankind's accountability to a Creator God.

Ironically, Daddy Darwin had wanted young Charlie to become a doctor or a clergyman, but it was not to be. He was in fact a nominal churchman until the death of his small daughter in 1851, when he "lost all faith in any sort of a benevolent God."[8]

In routine academic tradition and practice, scientific theories remain no more than that until proven. But Darwin's *Origin of the Species*, in contradiction to those accepted professional norms, *has never been proven*. Like-minded professionals over the years, in a snub to a God-ordered universe, tended to look the other way as others in opinionated-applause of Darwin's work, exalted the theory. But house-on-the-sand assumption is a far cry from credible research as scholarship is wont to require. Interestingly, a $250,000 prize has been offered by Dr. Kent Hovind of Creation Science Evangelism to anyone who could present credible proof of the Theory of Evolution.[9] Not surprisingly, no one has yet cashed in!

It is ironic how one Aristotle the Athenian, who dumped his mentor Plato's position on the supernatural as a legitimate source of knowledge, keeps popping up over and over again as we track throughout the ages the aftermath in this philosophical fork in the road.[10] It is chilling to realize how the influence of one man upon the legion of theologians and philosophers who followed, has now set the stage for a final showdown of the Judeo-Christian Heritage versus the Tree of Hellenistic Seduction—to be "clever like God" (review Gen. 3:1-7).

ENDNOTES

1. See: The Phrase Finder on http://www.phrases.org. uk/meanings/288200.html.

2. Thomas Hardy, English author (1840-1928), from the poem Christmas 1924: www.no1typo.me.uk/Christmas%201924.html.

3. Who2 on http://www.answers.com/topic/thomas-paine?hl = age&hl = reason.

4. Documented on www.answers.com. Recorded by Wikipedia; Isaac Newton, 5th Heading: Religious Views.

5. Documented on www.answers.com. Researched by Columbia University Press Encyclopedia; Descartes, René, Elements of Cartesian Philosophy, Paragraph 2.

6. Concise biographies of all four of these men are documented on www.answers.com and are quite readily researched.

7. "Public Opinion and the Media" by Paul Eidelberg, *Jerusalem Post*, Jan. 5, 1992.

8. Documented on www.answers.com. Recorded by Wikipedia under Charles Robert Darwin: Biography, under 5th Heading: *Family, work and development of theory.*

9. See Dr. Kent Hovind, Creation Science Evangelism; http://www.drdino.com.

10. Joseph Peiper, "Divine Madness": Plato's Case against Secular Humanism, http://www.amazon.com/exec/obidos/ASIN/0898705576/103-4484740-5517429.

CHAPTER SEVEN

JOHN DEWEY AND PONTIUS PILATE ON THE SAME PAGE

ALL Americans are probably a tad more than familiar with the now household name of the late Madalyn Murray O'Hair[1]. The name itself may not ring a bell to let her in the front door, but a "household" name nonetheless. She happens to be the agitated atheist who through legal petitioning to the United States Supreme Court, succeeded in 1963—along with a few like-minded financially fixed followers—to ban Bible reading as well as prayer in American public schools.

Now, this of course was a devious, less than democratic trick since, if a true poll were to be taken, those who have no particular grudge against God and His Good Book would have won by a landslide with realistic estimates as high as 80 percent or more. With that imbalance of loyalties, how did she manage to pull off this particular piece of perversion?

Well, the First Amendment of the United States Constitution states that, "Congress shall make no law respecting an establishment of religion or prohibiting the free exercise thereof." In my humble judgment, Ms. O'Hair, the Supreme Court, and millions of not-with-the-facts onlookers all made the same error of discernment. They didn't have a clue on the difference between "establishment of religion" and a "relationship."

Whether most dictionaries, most Christians, and the United States Supreme Court realize it or not, from Moses to Matthew, Mark, Luke and John, the faithful never presented their credentials to outsiders from the Baals to the Caesars or from Babylon to Rome. Their "establishment" of a creed was a statement of faith to Abba alone. So biblically, what's a religion? It's a relationship. But perhaps that's beside the point.

The way things are done these days obviously has slipped a cog with charters, registration, and the like. Nevertheless, the major point is that the American atheists are as much a religious organization as the Seventh Baptist Church of midtown America, except the atheists have a different god—a non-god. The summary is, therefore, that a little package of peanuts took their grievance against a much more voluminous package of popcorn to the Supreme Court about establishment of a "religion." And little peanuts won and thus were able to establish their religious preference to honor their non-god instead. Thanks to a judiciary that is far more learned in media judgments than it knows about Moses!

But it's not only the culpability of the courts. It is for this same kind of thinking that the Almighty is held in such low esteem throughout the Western world, because so much of the organized church have presumed themselves to either be God Himself, or at the least, His silver-tongued spokesperson. Obviously, those watching from the grandstands have not been all that impressed!

And it is for the same error in identity that the Islamic world thinks that Western morality is one and the same as Christianity. God have mercy on all those responsible for that blasphemous reflection!

Ironically, the early American Constitution was framed to guard against just this kind of mentality that the church itself is God, and therefore should be nicely equipped to run the show. Unfortunately, there appears to be far too much of a mist that clouds the difference between meaningful personal relationships to a higher power versus a dominating organized system of control. Of course, since 1963 all this has been infinitely rerun in the media—and on occasion in the courts. But it is vital that we tie it together here to get a clear overview on the moral mutiny that is happening around us, and the mind-set—or is it more the misleading manner—in which it is being done?

A mere 20 percent minority—undoubtedly even much fewer than that—has crept into the back door of the courtroom and snatched a judgment for themselves as the "preferred" religion to dominate the day. Get your God out of here because our god of godlessness has now barnacled itself to the big rudder instead. It is indefensible that atheism is not also a religious category. "Atheist" is a valid answer when filling out a document of any kind that asks the applicant to list his "religion." So instead of a battle of the morality being presented, it became *whose god*, and the atheists won!

And so did many other things, like lawlessness, high school massacres, drug abuse, family breakups, and myriads of perversions. Though atheism may not overtly teach these non-virtues, the lack of a solid moral foundation does. The baby has been jettisoned out of the Jacuzzi!

But wait a minute. All that the departed Madalyn Murray O'Hair had attained in her lifetime was flea dandruff compared to the bigger picture. Long before Madalyn's first legal maneuver in Baltimore, Maryland, a far more devastating mischief began to operate. Let's check that one out.

John Dewey (1859-1952), philosopher and educator, initiated a seemingly innocent but ultimately quantum shift in the American education system in the first half of the 20th century.

He introduced what he called "pragmatism" into the American psychology of teaching, which eventually influenced the rest of the West as well. So what's with pragmatism? What's wrong with teaching kids to be pragmatic, practical, realistic, that kind of thing? Sounds good. Why not?

On the other hand, perhaps we should check up on what else was in the pragmatic philosopher's planning. Pragmatic about what?

According to any quality encyclopedia, *pragmatism* means, "A method of philosophy in which the truth of a proposition is measured by its correspondence with experimental results and by its practical outcome."[2] The fine print, therefore, tells us that in Dewey's thinking the end results will either validate or invalidate the experimental means to get there. That is precariously close to the end justifying the means which flies directly into the face of bedrock values and principles—principles like the ones we find embedded in the Good Book.

More from our Columbia University Press Encyclopedia: "Pragmatism holds that *truth is modified* as discoveries are made and is relative to the time and place and purpose of inquiry." Did you get that? Ever hear of "situational ethics," the new morality bantered around since the '60s and even kicking around in the womb of new-wisdom long before that? Your circumstances dictate your behavior. It all depends on the situation. Absolutes have become archaic. They are no more. More Judeo-Christian bedrock is chipped away!

Moreover, Dewey would have us believe that truth is in the process of modification all the time. His commitment to pragmatism suggests that *truth is modified,* and what is true today may not be true tomorrow.[3]

But on the other side of the Tree of Knowledge, the one who has been referred to as the Son of Man declared, *"I am the...truth..."* (John 14:6), as well as, *"...know the truth and the truth will set you free"* (John 8:32). He was not boasting this as some human Well of Wisdom.com, but as a Right Arm representative of His Abba who sent Him, and who in turn had declared of Himself, *"I the LORD do not change..."* (Mal. 3:6). Thus we see a cosmic collision between these two diametrically opposed ideologies like has never yet occurred in outer space. Sadly, it has long since occurred in American classrooms as well as all such similar laboratories of learning across the Western world. Shall we say that truth has become the Play-dough of humanism!

Dewey likewise takes a dim view of history, suggesting that teaching history to kids is a waste of time. It has little "pragmatic" value since what happened in the past has no bearing on where we ought to be looking for the future. Somehow I much prefer—and more than concur—with another noted philosopher, George Santayana, whose take on the value of history is far more reasonable, as well as self-evident from practice: "Those who cannot remember the past are condemned to repeat it."[4]

That also underlines for me in red that an otherwise well-intentioned professor Dewey wouldn't care all that much for my Bible either. That of course details the foundation of Hebraic history, which in turn is the bedrock of the Creator's revelation of historical truth. And to weave together all the threads, according to Dewey's bio in Wikipedia, he held little credence—actually none at all to be exact—in the Abba of Abraham Himself.[5]

Unfortunately Dewey, like legions of other less than clued-in onlookers, reckoned that the Bible is a sort of religious rulebook. It's *not*—not unless, of course, you have read that incorrect assumption into it through a Hellenist philosophy filter. When we read it with a Hebraic mind-set, the Good Book rather becomes a historical record of God's interaction with His creation. That means that not all of it is nice and rosy—like you and I are not all nice and rosy. But I recall that those who yearn to learn from the past will be, after all, less inclined to repeat it. And from my long-term tenure of keeping an eye on the long-term results—I use different measurement standards than Dewey to be sure—I find that Abba's promises are more than true and are not likely to change as the sun sets.

So let's go back to this "truth" concept that Dewey denied existed in the long term. It was a skeptical Pontius Pilate who asked our renowned Rabbi from Galilee if he was the King of the Jews, and in the recorded course of the cross-examination, Yeshua replied that He *"...came into the world, to testify to the truth."* (John 18:37b). (Dewey would have done a back flip on that one as well!) To that,

Pilate cynically asked Him, *"What is truth?"* (John 18:38a), which put him on the same page as educator Dewey, since the problematic philosopher didn't seem to have a clue either.

The only thing I have to say about Pontius P, however, is that later on as the sky grew black and the scenario even blacker, he had actually ordered the inscription *"King of the Jews"* to identify the condemned Yeshua as He died. And he refused to change it, even at the turbulent pressure of the hate-driven horde of protesters. So, all in all, maybe something about *truth* did filter through to the hard-bitten Roman boss after all. Who knows?

But not so to the American educator of the early 20th century! He stuck with his philosophy that reality changes like the morning dew, and with her morals now crashing down like a hailstorm, America—not to mention the rest of the West—sadly got stuck with his philosophy!

And stuck with more than that. For at least three generations of "pragmatic" education, the Western World has been condemned to relativism, situation ethics, and experimental social science. And Dewey's experimental toying with human life has deteriorated in turn to an uncontrolled corruption of cultural values, a meltdown of social mores, disintegration of family structure, delinquency, drugs, and all manner of test-it-out relationships. An utterly sick society ultimately tests not only positive to the virus of Hellenistic humanism, but more than that, as a terminally ill counter-culture cursed with godlessness! The text we quoted back in Chapter One bears repeating:

> *Woe to those who call evil good and good evil, who put darkness for light and light for darkness, who put bitter for sweet and sweet for bitter. Woe to those who are wise in their own eyes and clever in their own sight* (Isaiah 5:20-21).

In science we conduct experiments for the technical progress of posterity, but in an educational foray that experiments with young human lives, when Humpty Dumpty crashes, "all the king's horses and all the king's men" are as helpless and hopeless as hapless

Humpty! But where now are those experimenting social engineers to reverse this distressing descent to anarchy? The truth is that we are long past any easy answers, and those secular "lifeguards" of our times have sadly never learned how to swim themselves!

If Darwin—aside from any worthwhile naturalist discoveries—pulled the rug from under a Creator God to whom all humanity is accountable, then Dewey in turn made his own philosophical gamble to deftly chip away the bedrock from under the Almighty's universal principles of truth. Dewey not only lost the bet, but as we now view for ourselves his "pragmatic" test results, a morally empty-handed Western society has lost everything else!

And we wonder why the world's ethics, justice, and morals are in such a chaotic morass today? Madalyn did her destructive bit, but it was merely a fragment. Worldwide apostasy and corruption have been in an incubation stage for a long, long time with Hellenistic seeds being planted as far back as those anti-Hebraic origins of humanism. But even further back than that, we began with that lingering lust for power in the Garden—to be simply clever like God!

But while we're on to experimenting with human lives, Dewey reflected on one other experiment in human destiny—that of democracy. "The test of a democracy, Dewey believed, is the degree to which all people likely to suffer the consequences of a decision, have (themselves) participated in the making of that decision."[6] Behold, democracy *could be made* to serve an honest, cooperative society well, as much or more than any other human political system. But to remove the honesty and cooperation, and to replace it with duplicity, greed for wealth, and lust for power is, my friends, the Achilles' heel of any democratic system ever conceived. When a colossal bridge is poorly designed, scores perhaps will eventually die. When an abused and misused political system—even an initially good system—is tried and found wanting, an entire cultural era will perish from the earth! Though the likes of John Dewey may prefer to look the other way, it has happened before!

Take the Islamic inclination to "play" the democratic game long enough to create the numbers to "democratically" vote in Shari'a law, or a "democratic" annihilation of Israel, or any other dubious long-term agenda, and you have a classic example of Dewey's proposed learn-from-your-errors human experimentation. Is this not the magnificent Holy Grail of democracy the West is so futilely chasing in the Middle East? Have you checked the MEMRI[7] translations of sermons in the Mosques recently? And we hardly mean merely those Al Qaeda threats and boasts! Perhaps it never occurred to John Dewey that there is a point of no return both in the Middle East and in the inner cities of the globe with a mindless experimentation with human lives.

Unfortunately, Mr. Dewey fantasized human experiments in democracy as a legitimate direction where people learn from making bad decisions. Indeed, more scrambled Humpty Dumpty. Thanks, but no thanks! Well-meaning but shortsighted educator Dewey may have egg on his post-humus face. Suffice it to say that his pragmatic system of education is—like shattered Humpty—hardly what it is cracked up to be!

In his metaphor for pursuing *"wisdom, discipline, and understanding,"* Solomon the wise said, *"Buy the truth and do not sell it"* (Prov. 23:23).

Pontius Pilate sold it for a few cheap political points; John Dewey gave it away! And since then the Western educational system in general, and the American secular education system in particular, have been gearing up, for not a few decades now, in shaping a truth-free curriculum for a less than promising New World Order.

ENDNOTES

1. Violently murdered along with a son and an adopted granddaughter by underworld figures, presumably for her money. See http://crimemagazine.com/ohair.htm.

2. Columbia University Press Encyclopedia. http://www.answers.com/Pragmatism.

3. John Dewey, See WHO2; Columbia University Press Encyclopedia; Wikipedia; all accessed on: http://www.answers.com/John%20Dewey.

4. George Santayana, The Life of Reason or Phases of Human Progress, 82; Charles Scribner's Sons, New York, 1954.

5. John Dewey; Wikipedia under Deweyan pragmatism; http://www.answers.com/John%20Dewey.

6. John Dewey: Biography by Houghton Mifflin Company; http://www.answers.com/John%20Dewey.

7. Middle East Media Research Institute: http://memri.org.

CHAPTER EIGHT

THE DECLARATION OF HUMAN WRONGS

OKAY. So I borrowed the title and turned it just a tad from the Universal Declaration of Human Rights that was adopted and proclaimed by the General Assembly resolution 217A (III) of December 10, 1948.

After the incomprehensible carnage of World War II in which up to 80 million lives were wantonly lost—counting some 57 million civilians including those 6 million Jews—the kings of the earth merged their minds to ban this kind of catastrophic calamity from ever occurring again. So they summoned their best brains together, and for starters they came up with a document they called the Universal Declaration of Human Rights.

And here's what they said that everyone was supposed to do with it:

> On December 10, 1948 the General Assembly of the United Nations adopted and proclaimed the Universal Declaration of Human Rights, the full text of which appears in the following pages. Following this historic act the Assembly called upon all Member countries to publicize the text of the Declaration and "to cause it to be disseminated, displayed, read and expounded principally in schools and other educational institutions

without distinction based on the political status of countries or territories.

That's interesting. They're chasing after those school kids again!

Actually, if even the kids are supposed to read it, I suggest you read the full Declaration as well. Most of it is not too bad. You can pick it up on the web and see for yourself what they put together.[1]

There are only a few problems, however:

1) The document—most of it anyway—declares what society ideally should be like in a sort of reinvented Garden of God. Sad to say, any mention of the Guardian of the garden gate, or should we say King of the Universe, is deafening in its silence.

2) It splendidly lists the suggested idealistic treatment of all humanity—including freedom of "religion or belief."[2] Unfortunately, the much-revered holy books of the globe's fastest growing religion—books that demand unqualified obedience by over one-sixth of the world's population—undeniably declare that the infidel (read: Jews and Christians) must be eliminated, which suggests a snag before we even get started.

3) Moreover, it is the fundamentalist mainstream of this massive segment of religious oppression that has now managed to gain an immense influence on global human-ity by means of political tools ranging from oil supply to terrorist threats. And much of that terrorist intimidation deals with outright anti-Semitic propaganda and Hitler-like cries to cleanse the world of Jews once and for all. This can be confirmed by merely taking note of the roughly 10-to-1 support by the "non-aligned nations" (read: Islamic block) in those routine condemnations of tiny Israel in United Nations General Assembly voting records. The Arabs primarily initiate approximately 20 of these routine Israel-bashing resolutions per year, and this

has spanned the last four decades or even longer. Check it out.

Tragically, no government of the globe has the intestinal fortitude to face up to the real root of the problem. (They all drive cars that run on petroleum!) Thus far, an inoffensive euphemism, "War on Terror" has been coined to soften the bite on those nations who are directly or indirectly linked to hatred of Jews. Yet these are the very ones who scramble for front-row seats, in order to be the first to hear those self-righteous echoes from the Universal Drama of Human Rights. And the cancer spreads.

Could the 21st century offspring of the ancient Hebrews who gave us the concept of a Creator God and His Scriptures really be that bad? Or is the Islamic block (now read in reverse: non-aligned nations) really that intellectually handicapped to presume that a minute 0.2 percent of the world's population could be that much of a menace to their well being? The Declaration unequivocally states, "rights, freedom and protection for all." How then can it be that the "non-aligned" along with the oil-soaked Western allies with their crude cause, not infrequently funnel their General Assembly voices into the hatred for, and denigration of, the Jewish people?

Though this is a bit of an aside from the direction we want to go in this chapter, it exposes from the start the blatant hypocrisy of the Declaration of Human Rights that was formulated to finally fix all of humanity's problems of prejudice, deprivation, and inequality. As George Orwell said it so eloquently in *Animal Farm*, "All animals are equal, but some animals are more equal than others."[3]

Something smells extremely bad, and especially so since this was the diabolical scheme of the Nazi agenda from 1938-1945 to eliminate world Jewry from the face of the earth in a pretense of effecting a Jewish-free "economic stability" as well as genetic cleansing for "racial quality." If you burrow back into the history of World War II, the Arab Muslims were the only major unrepentant allies of Adolph Hitler. Moreover, also note that there were no war-crimes trials for Hitler's enthusiasts in the Middle East in general and the Islamic Mufti from Jerusalem in particular. They just went back home licking their ideological wounds when their hero of Jew-hatred was shot dead by the advancing Russian troops. There is no shortage of records from those days, except that the media misplaced their files, and global governments have more important things to do than pretending that Jews are more significant than Arab oil.

But besides that, there is one other discreditable faux pas that we must examine even more closely as we check up on the accuracy of the moral high-ground of the UN Declaration of 1948. The focus of the Human Rights Pronouncement is on what *ought* to be done to alleviate the pain of the suffering masses among us, but not one iota of insight into *who* exactly is going to do it, *how* it might be carried out, or probably most significant of all, *how* did it ever get to be in such a dreadful state of injustice and inequality in the first place?

Without question, global equality and human well being are now in unimaginable collapse—far greater than could ever have been conceived in 1948. I have no quarrel against Band-aids—they are an ingenious invention; but Band-aids were never meant for cancer. Worse yet, the Supreme Surgeon General has long been kicked out of His hospital. Never has the world needed His ingenious expertise and adept scalpel as it does in these days of approaching anarchy.

The virus causing this tragic moral morass, even though spawned from as far back as the fifth century B.C., has yet to be recognized and diagnosed as Hellenistic humanism. And without the foggiest notion as to the terminal nature of the disease, the tranquilizer prescribed by the United Nations has been "Human Rights."

These next three chapters are the most pivotal in my whole book, because the United Nations' mentality and influence are whirling all around us from cell phone to Internet, and from the media to the mailbox. Most people don't pay that much attention, because the UN isn't exactly their favorite contact sport or tea party topic. Nor are the dreary political platitudes from those threadbare

Geneva Conventions any more inspirational than a flat tire on the freeway.

That's the problem. The issues we're going to look at in these next few chapters are in actual fact involved in that whirlpool we call 21st-century survival. They influence our current mind-set as well as our down-to-earth direction. Yet the irony is that we hardly know what it is that is daily twisting our arms, not to mention the ancient garbage pits from which these influences have long since wormed their way into what we had presumed was our own private lives.

I think the first mention I ever heard of human rights was back somewhere in the '70s from Jimmy Carter when he was President of the United States. I probably wasn't listening too well before then, but when Carter began using the terminology, it in some way caught my attention—possibly my curiosity. Somehow it didn't quite ring true, but I was not sure why.

Perhaps it was because when I left the nuclear laboratory in 1957 to do a bit more promising things than chasing plutonium particles, I read a small book to help prepare my wife and me for an intriguing but precarious new career of linguistics and Bible translation in the once Stone Age wilds of Papua New Guinea. The book was entitled, *Have We No Right?*[4] and was written by some obscure missionary lady whose prettiest shoes were without a doubt designed for hiking hills, and who probably never tried on a formal in her whole life.

The gist of her message was that if we are on assignment for the King, *we have no rights.* Depending on the role for which we have been designed, there are those who may never have the opportunity to get married, to have a family, or even to have amenable housing for any length of time. In short, toughing it out between a rock of conviction and a hard place of carrying it out, you may not be privileged to have all the other good stuff in this life that "normal" people have. Putting it that way, "normal" people might well suggest those Christians not "on assignment" for the King...wait a minute; maybe I'd better start that line over!

Anyway Carter, and all those Presidents who followed him kept talking about these nations with hopeless human rights records, and if they would only come up to standard, the U.S.A. would do business with them (read: make a good profit). Now, encouraging other nations to shape up in how they treat their unfortunates is not a bad principle to follow—presuming, of course, that you have treated your own early primitive folks in praiseworthy fashion!

But the strange thing is that for some decades now, Saudi Arabia has rarely been mentioned, and if they were, it was never too loud. Of course, we all know that all nations like to do business with any country that has the largest oil reserves in the world. Obviously, I take this to mean that the Saudis must have a flawless human rights record with all levels of Saudi society, (including terrorists). Never mind those infidels of Judeo-Christian heritage! In fact, the Saudi government is so protective of Christians that it warns them not to try to bring a Bible into the country, which wisdom will spare them from their pesky police who would otherwise pounce upon them and thrust them into jail! For that matter, I have heard that their jails are not all that human rights friendly either. But Saudi Arabia has never been a problem for Jews. That is, I've never heard of any Jews yet that would take the chance to go there!

So I've been thinking this thing of human rights through for many years now, and even though the United Nations is such an august and upright body without a taint of bias or hypocrisy (whoops), I now venture to make my own declaration that their well-meaning perception of human rights is wrong—very wrong.

Why? There's certainly nothing wrong with being sensitive to the desperate needs of a suffering globe. That's a good thing. In fact, it's a God-thing. We need to be involved. But the Almighty calls it *"justice,"* not rights. "Justice" puts the Most High in the driver's seat where He belongs, and us a servant to that cause. "Rights," on the other hand, elevates humankind into that humanistic control tower of demanding right from wrong. And that is wrong!

And the whole world has swallowed the pill without even thinking to check for the side effects and the use-by date, which happens—in this case—to be Gen.03.05. Strange I never heard of a month named "Gen" before? Must be one of those funny sounding Hebrew months!

Classically, in April 2002, Kofi Anan, the then Secretary General of the United Nations, posed the question, "Can Israel be right and all the world be wrong?"

Indeed, Mr. Anan, they can be. Not exactly the Israelis, Mr. Anan, because some of them can be as corrupt and sanitized from their Hebraic roots as anyone else on earth. But the God of Israel who has had an impeccable record for accuracy over the millennia, brought the scattered outcasts of Israel back to their ancient homeland in the late 1800s in a fulfillment of over 90 specific biblical prophecies. And very significantly, we would do well to note that in those days, it was to a very sparsely populated land that He brought them back.[5]

Moreover, He ultimately ratified their return in 1948 by awarding them their own State, ironically under the very nose of the UN. What is more, it seems the Eternal One always will have the last word, regardless of what Washington, Paris, London, Moscow, or even the UN Security Council says. In fact, that is what the Bible— the record of the God of creation—is all about. *"Then they will know that I Am the LORD"* (Ezek. 36:38b)[6] is repeated some 80 times in the Hebrew Scriptures.

So, as I had mused over this candy-flavored human rights thing for many years, one day I was inspired to probe the bedrock of what the Good Book said about the subject. Guess what! I found that the General Assembly didn't get their clues from Abraham, Moses, or even Yeshua on their various pronouncements. They started out by chipping a bit of Isaiah's prophecy on the marble exterior of the UN building in New York, *"They will beat their swords into plowshares and their spears into pruning hooks. Nation will not take up sword against nation, nor will they train for war anymore"* (Isa. 2:4b). But once that was chiseled into stone, it seemed to be the end of any Hebraic usefulness to the United Nations.

So what *does* the Bible say about human rights? Not much at all—in fact, zero. It probably says more by omission, than by mention. The Scriptures speak rather of *human responsibilities* from beginning to end.

The nearest thing you can find on "human rights" in the Good Book is Lamentations 3:35 which, in shifting the rhetorical question into a statement declares, *'[The Lord will not]...deny a man his rights before the Most High, to deprive a man of justice..."* (Lam. 3:35-36). That's the closest and only Scripture that comes anywhere near mentioning the UN heralded and currently politically correct concept of "human rights." But even then, in that same verse, several other translations use the word "privilege" instead of "rights," while yet one other translation uses "justice." So in the sum of it, the only possible biblical suggestion of "rights" is that all of humanity has a "right" to stand before their God. Sounds good enough for me, and for all others who are close enough on the inside track to know what kind of a daddy that Abba is.

As we noted in Chapter One, in linguistics, it is not the *likeness* of two similar words that is important, but rather where those two words *differ* in meaning.[7] It so happens that there are several other mentions in Scripture of the "right to" or "rights," especially in the New International or the New King James Versions.[8] However, careful examination of these occurrences will reveal that the basic meaning involved is not the "demanding of a claim" but rather ministering to a need, the "pleading of a cause," a "fair judgment," or "honest decision" by an overseeing authority.

The reality rather, is basically going to God to request defense from an antagonist—seen or unseen—who designs to take advantage. These are pleas for a controlling hand from Above, and definitely not the demanded "rights" concepts of the General Assembly Declaration. Supernatural sovereignty has been crassly cropped from the photograph!

A word-study analysis of the fine-tuned meaning of "human rights" is that the one who makes his declaration has a legitimate demand-authority over whoever else it is that is supposed to be providing it—the state, the society, or other human beings. Therefore, when I declare my "rights," it signifies that I presume to hold leverage over another who had better come through or else. Thus, that puts him under my dominance—which even includes the God who "holds the whole wide world in His hands."

It sounds like the same old saga of the selection that Slippery Sam offered us in the Garden scenario back in Chapter One. Do you have any added advice for us at this point, Mrs. Adam's?

By contrast, a need or cause implies that someone of higher capability has either a responsibility or an opportunity to cover the bases for a friend in need who can use a bit of help. My cause, my need, or my petition for an honest hearing semantically means that there is someone above me to whom I can turn for the Hebraic concept of help, instead of the humanistic charter of demand. Most often, this is yet another earthling in any and all levels of society, not to forget the fact that the Almighty still has His hand on the happenings that hover above their heads as well.

In any case, filing the initial request would realistically be directly through Abba's office, to whom we can go without embarrassment, without hesitation, and invariably, without disappointment, because He has strings to pull that you wouldn't believe. On the other hand, it's better you do believe it!

"Rights" imply claim and control. "Needs" imply dependency, or actually, interdependency since we all are in continually shifting roles of either need for ourselves, or for the responsibility to assist others within the human family.

So in summary, human rights are anything but a biblical concept. Rather, the Good Book gives us *human responsibilities*, in how we should look out for one another. The Torah—the five Books of Moses—repeatedly teach the Hebraic community how to care for everyone from extended family to the "alien who dwells among you." And the New Covenant repeatedly reiterates to *"Love your neighbor as yourself"* (Lev. 19:18; Matt. 5:43; 19:19), and adds in one case, *"Consider others better than yourselves"* (Rom. 12:10; Phil. 2:3).

So the concept that we humans have "rights" hardly came from the Hebraic side of the Great Divide. Quite the opposite. We have an Abba who more than cares, more than provides, and appears unfair only because we have somehow developed our own insights on how the Great Designer might improve His performance to better steer the universe to our advantage at the moment! (Did I get that right, Mrs. Adam's?)

Unfortunately, most Westerners—and not the least, much of the presumed Bible-believing, no-nonsense Christianity within the Western World—have become such scrambled eggs of syncretism into a Hellenistic lifestyle that they are oblivious to the fact that their train has long ago whistled past their station. Sadly, the next stop is not exactly where they had intended to get off! Intermingled with self-deluding doctrinal clichés, devoid of an all-important intimacy with the Most High, the majority have not the slightest clue how deeply entrenched they already are into the seductive mind-set of a New World Order. Did I hear someone out there say "antichrist"?

If God is anything unique from any and all of His challengers— from the gods of the Canaanites to a 21st century Global Village that no longer wants Him—He is *"justice, mercy, and faithfulness,"* (Matt. 23:23; Mic. 6:8), the character portrait He reflects throughout the Scriptures. And those who have never seen that reflection probably don't know Abba.

Actually, that's what this book is all about. Hellenism is looking at the King of the Universe through the wrong end of the telescope!

ENDNOTES

1. http://www.unhchr.ch/udhr/lang/eng.htm.

2. Ibid., See Article 18.

3. AUTHOR – Insert documentation for George Orwell, Animal Farm.

4. Mabel Williamson, *Have We No Right?* (London: China Inland Mission; Lutterworth Press, 1958).

5. See two articles: *The Demise of Distorting History*, http://www.spim.org.au/articles/article3.doc; and Who Occupies Whose Land? http://www.spim.org.au/article4.htm posted under Articles on the South Pacific Island Ministries Website, http://www.spim.org.au.

6. With a similar concept occurring some 60 times in Ezekiel, and more than 20 additional references throughout the Hebrew (Old Testament) Scriptures.

7. See also an additional reference to this principle in Chapter One.

8. Interestingly, these two translations were both done *after* the shifting world mind-set following the UN Declaration, which raises the question whether this had been an influence in word choice contrasting with other much earlier translations.

CHAPTER NINE

The Child, The Lady, and Life in the Beehive

As my son-in-law was sitting in his car in torrid and steaming Belem, Brazil, with his arm hanging out the window (Brazilian air-con style), waiting for the traffic light to change, a young kid came roaring past, ripped off his wristwatch, and ran for all he was worth.

He was a street kid—no home, no family to speak of, and he probably had no idea who his father was, or at least *where* he was. Scott's wristwatch became the lad's food for the next few days.[1]

Street kids—Brazil is full of them. So is almost every major city spanning the globe in both the Western and undeveloped nations of the world. No home—no dad—no future—and no hope.

Except for one city that I know well in the South Pacific—Port Moresby, the capital of Papua New Guinea where we spent a 30-year tenure in Bible translation and related spiritual and community ministry.

Hold it. Don't get me wrong. Port Moresby is a dangerous place—complete with crime and armed robbery as with any other inner city—but what I said was "no street kids." There are no "orphans" in PNG, as well as most other nations of the Pacific Islands. Every son has a fistful of fathers. If his birth dad is gone, he has an extended family of uncles, elder brothers, or even cousins, to take a departed father's place. He *belongs* somewhere because the once animist, now Christian Pacific nations, have escaped the Greek humanist aftermath of the nuclear family and reflect instead the Hebraic culture of the extended family. Indeed, Papua New Guinea has plenty of other problems, but street kids are not among them.

Enter the United Nations' *Convention of Rights of the Child* from November 20, 1989.

Now, in spite of my insistence in our previous chapter that it's a bit one-eyed to call them "rights" instead of "needs," the 54-Article treatise is not too bad as long as you substitute "needs" instead of "rights" across the document. If you're a lawyer or politician or someone of that level of legality, you might enjoy looking it up on the net.[2] They're doing their best to look out after the kids.

But look, when we can view videos copied directly from Palestinian Authority TV, showing four-year old suicide-trainee Palestinian kids being exhibited with mock suicide belts and real rifles longer than they are tall, one's blood curdles.[3]

When we see news clips of African infants dying of AIDS or malnutrition with flies crawling in and out of their open mouths, our hearts are wrenched. We can't even look!

Or bits of flesh from Jewish children plastered against the sides of buildings adjacent to a blast from the vitriolic hatred of suicide bombers, you get sick in the stomach.

Or 12-year-old Asian girls who have been abducted into a life of sex slavery in Southeast Asia—or anywhere else in the world. Can you visualize your daughter locked into that hell?

So the 1989 UN Convention on the Rights of the Child has tried hard—no one can fault them for their effort.

Except for a few things they overlooked.

By Intelligent Design from the beginning, along with a few clues from Moses, Yeshua, and friends, to focus on the needs of the kids is not the most productive plan on the table. It's the duties of a dad! Where are the fertility factories that fathered these unfortunates?

Those good intentions of the 1989 Convention for the welfare of children have told the nations very clearly and specifically what *ought to be done* for the world's suffering youngsters.

But they have not told us:

1) Done by whom?

2) Why are the kids disadvantaged in the first place?

3) Who is responsible for creating their demise?

4) And above all, how does the globe get back to basics?

You can't get back to basics by booting out the God of creation even before you begin, because you are afraid of offending:

1) Those who have a skewed concept—if any concept at all—of the Designer.

2) Those who have an alternate agenda for their own god, which happens to feature violence and political control but *not* the needs of kids.

3) Religious leaders—including Christians—who are more politicians than shepherds.

4) Religious leaders—especially Christians—who wouldn't know Abba if they saw Him.

Okay. Facts are facts. But with the globe tottering on the sheer edge of anarchy, it's a bit naïve to think of searching for the sire of the kid who ripped off my son-in-law's wristwatch. It may be a bit late! But Scripture also says, *"Strengthen the things which remain..."* (Rev. 3:2 KJV).

And what does the Almighty say further to those families who keen to survive, are yet precariously close to being sucked into the sewage system of humanistic futility? *"Train a child in the way he should go,*[4] *and when he is old he will not turn from it"* (Prov. 22:6); *"Folly is bound up in the heart of a child, but the rod of discipline will drive it far from him"* (Prov. 22:15); and "Fathers do not exasperate your children; instead, bring them up in the training and instruction of the Lord" (Eph. 6:4). And I'm sure if you've come with me thus far in this get-it-together-with-Abba book, you also realize that when we look back, most of us see things now that we wished we had seen back then. And unfortunately, even now, most of us know a lot more of what we ought to do—or even wish we could do—than we are actually able to keep up with on the performance side. But hang in there; with Abba's help we'll make it. A family who prays together *to* Abba will be provided for together *by* Abba.

And the Jews? It's been said that Jews—that is, the God-fearing Jews—don't keep the Sabbath, but it's the Sabbath that keeps the Jews.

A lot of Christians are not too clued in on what the Abba-oriented Jews do on Saturday, but I've found out that it's not so much what they do—or don't do—on Saturday, but what they really do on Friday night as the sun sets. It's a family circle traditionally designed to relate to the Almighty, and every child in the family is to receive a personal blessing by their earthly abba. And as old Tevye says in *Fiddler on the Roof,* "Everyone knows who he is, and what God expects of him."

So much for what the world's kids need. They need an Abba—in lieu of an abba in absentia—and those of us committed to Judeo-Christian beginnings know that we must start from there. It's not some doleful UN document of what needs to be done, but a life-illuminating relationship with the One who alone can effect it.

But when a humanist society awards Dad his "rights" to run away from his responsibilities for some sex siren on another street, what can we expect?

And now ladies, this next probe of improprieties is what you have been waiting for—especially those of you who have seemingly been shortchanged by a male-dominated society up until now. Let's have a look at women's rights, or shall we call it, "Life in the Beehive"?

I'm not even going to get into the General Assembly *Convention on the Elimination of All Forms of Discrimination against Women* of December 1979. For that matter, perhaps journalist Gloria Steinem and the late author Betty Freiden have declared it even more authoritatively than the less than stimulating UN proclamations. From what I have researched, both authors, in being the prime initiators of the feminist movement, have eased to much more moderate positions in recent years. Not to worry, however, for our more fanatic friends. A new generation of fighting femmies has been raising the steaks (no spelling error here), to the point where men must now do their own barbequing!

Look ladies, when it comes to voting, property rights, equal pay for equal work, being cheapened into sex images, I'm on your side. But what I want to look into here is not the degradation that has been forced upon the female of the species over millennia, but whodunit? Only by knowing why your car engine is clunking so dreadfully are you able to fix it. If you come up with the whys, you don't necessarily have to go out and trade in your old junk for a newer version that may be even tinnier than the old-faithful that started making the funny noises.

For starters, gals, you didn't become heir to your Western world exploitation cum insecurities—or for some, mistreatment from Middle Eastern inhumanities—from the Hebraic side of the valley. It just could be that today's less than sensitive and competitive-style males picked up their tactless masculine manners from the other side of the Great Divide.

In their highly touted "learning" gymnasiums, the Hellenists mixed their sexes together, delicately clad in the same skin in which they were born. These flesh-toned "school uniforms" made do from pre-puberty well into adulthood. From the hopefully scholastic study halls to sports-hour somersaults, the Greeks sought to idolize the human body—all of it—as the ultimate of beauty!

Perversion was the name of the game. Since the schoolyard bully never seems to be the scrawniest kid in the class, it shouldn't take a doctorate in physiology to figure out where male bigotry got an uninhibited start, and why it perpetuates itself throughout the Western world to this day. What's more, can you comprehend what the corresponding jibes from the locker-room mentality of the day did to a growing girl's self-image? Zits would be a piece of cake compared to the uninhibited and far more cruel schoolboy taunts of those "educational" forays.

And then, ladies, mull this one over! I've just been going through a rundown of the Greek philosophers recently. How many of that prestigious *all-male lineup* do you think were women? Fasten your seatbelts, gals; the seeds of Hellenism throughout the Western World's hothouses of chauvinism have hit harvest time!

So for any and all who reckon that the Creator is the culprit, or that the Bible beleaguers the beauties among us, let's now have a look at the Hebraic ideals.

Four matriarchs in the Abrahamic family of promise and redemption are honored throughout the Scriptures.

Deborah in the Book of Judges was a prophetess, a judge, and *the* leader of Israel, who with a fist of steel—and the help of another housewife, Jael—delivered Israel from their oppressors in her day (see Judges 4:1-24). Not to offend my friends in the United Kingdom, but Judge Debbie made the Iron Lady of London look like a schoolgirl!

And then there was Ruth the Moabitess who switched sides in an allegiance to Abba and got an upgrade to first class on her flight into Bethlehem (see Ruth 1:1–4:22).

Queen Esther majestically saved her people when an alert Uncle "Moti" reversed a nasty plot for Jewish genocide, and—as did Ruth—even now has a Book of the Bible named after her (see Esther 2:1–9:32).

A young girl named Miriam (it's Mary in English) from Nazareth in Upper Galilee was chosen as a mother for the King of the Jews (see Luke 1:26-38).

A demon-possessed casualty named Miriam (again read: Mary) from Magdala, whose Hebrew claim to fame was overcoming the occult, now holds an extremely honored heritage in Judeo-Christian recognition (see Luke 8:1-3; Matt. 27:55-56).

And finally, there is the story of the wayward woman who blew it big-time in an illicit affair, and whom the big boys on the religious council caught out "to make her an example" (see John 8:3-11). Yeshua returned her to decency. (He came from the Hebraic side of things, remember?) Her accusers have long since been scattered and forgotten, but she remains immortalized as a woman who morally silenced the cynics.

So that's a bit of a taste of Hebraic appreciation for but a few of the highly featured females from the Good Book.

And we've been cruising along fairly smoothly on this Hebraic freeway up to now, but I do see some construction up ahead that might slow us down a bit—but only marginally.

In the Brit Hadasha—the New Covenant Scriptures—we do run into a few problem passages primarily by apostle Paul, but a bit by Peter as well, that could serve to slow us slightly for a tad of linguistic research. In no way am I going to convene a Bible study at this point on what the ladies should look like, how much they dare say in the sanctuary, or how low to bow to the brilliant mentality of men. It's going to be much, much simpler than that. We're on a freeway, remember.

I merely suggest we switch our Hellenistic spectacles for Hebraic cultural contact lenses. Reading Paul with traditional Western thinking, the Hellenized mind-set may give jabs like, "*dumb woman!*" whereas a Hebraic mind-set paints an altogether different landscape.

Perhaps the most classic example of all such trip-up texts is in Paul's first letter to young Timothy (see 1 Tim. 2:9-15), with prickly present-day terms like "full submission"; "silence is golden, sister"; "the woman was deceived" (see Gen. 3:5-6); and "saved through child bearing"—quick turn the page!

With a bit of Greek gymnasium mentality, it doesn't take long to forget those holy heroines on the last couple of pages.

So let's go further back to the Garden scenario in Genesis.

The word chosen to represent her deed of disobedience (for which Adam promptly followed suit) in the New Covenant text is "deceived." That is the Greek word that is used, to be sure, and that root terminology is translated quite the same in English. However, with a closer examination of the cultural context combined with the root meaning, I suggest a far better rendering would be "attacked." This throws an entirely new Hebraic light into the whole drama. Deception, of course, is still a significant component of the term "attack." Thus, this verse in Timothy might more meaningfully read, *"And Adam was not* [attacked]; *it was the woman who was* [attacked] *and became* [disobedient]" (1 Tim. 2:14). I see no "dumb woman" option of understanding here. Rather, it's "pity the poor gal."

But why was it the woman? The attack was hardly because she was merely a soft target, but for the remarkable reality of *who she actually was*.

The woman had been uniquely designed as the cradle of *chai* (Hebrew for *life*), the Eternal Architect's most classic creation to guarantee His ongoing plan for life. It would appear that His "Friday afternoon" finishing touch of creation was His supreme surprise package for Adam. The woman was the Creator's divine blueprint for the perpetuation of *chai*.

Womanhood, therefore, had been exalted as the original Miss Universe, not merely for her outward beauty, but for the model Proverbs 31 woman of valor: *"Who can find a virtuous woman? for her price is far above rubies"* (Prov. 31:10 KJV). The word translated as "virtuous" or sometimes "noble character" means far more in Hebrew than those limited expressions in English. The deeper reflections of the Hebrew root are that she embodies the inner strength and courage of an army. She is the Creator's choice moral fiber in designing this channel of beauty and dignity for His highest and most sensitive role that assures continuity of His human family.

Moreover, Adam was posted as her security guard to see that nothing happened to Queen Bee. In the hive, the queen bee merits multi-thousands of protectors, but as close as Adam was to Abba, he should have been able to handle it by himself. However, one morning he slept in and whammo—Mrs. Adam's became easy pickings for Slippery Sam! And here we are! You know the rest of the story.

Now transfer this insight into Paul's closing comments in his letter to Timothy. *"But women will be saved through childbearing"* (1 Tim. 2:15a). A better rendering through the cultural insights just given may be, "But womanhood will be preserved for continuity of the creation at all costs," even when overseer Adam may be caught napping on occasion. This verse has nothing to do with women having babies individually or having babies in order to be "saved." But it has everything to do with the Creator's mega-value on His prized dynamic of womanhood. And the last half of the verse finishes with an "if" clause. In a very broad concept, if the woman commits herself to a godly life, she becomes an honor to the exalted female status that the Creator had initially awarded her.

Nor is this to ever say that her role would be all glitz and glamour. The Almighty told her that her childbearing would be painful, and that her husband's role would be tough sledding as well (see Gen. 3:16-19). No majestic mountain is ever conquered—and I have stood on top of a few in my day—without not a little pain and perseverance. Life is a gift, given for whatever seemingly impossible role we have been designed, and into whatever untenable surroundings we may have been planted. And Abundant Life is our choice to hit the tape sprinting, no matter who we may happen to be.

But our bottom line must be to once-and-for-all knock down that abominable status ladder that has been erected through the Hellenistic hero worship of a peck-order, and to return to an Abba-ordained sense of equality and justice for the entire family that feasts at the table of the King.

Male authority is a corresponding designer gift for faithful men as a covering of protection over His priceless cradle of life. We men are not superior—that's a Hellenistic hiccup. But we are most often made as the physically stronger of the team and generally with built-in talents of leadership. However, if men opt out and don't use the gifts God gave them, by all means let the Hebraic-oriented

Deborah's move in! We all have seen some absolutely fabulous beauty queens whose measurements excel in the virtues of valor, character, inner strength, and the courage of an army!

And for that S-word used both in the writings of Paul and Peter— "cooperation" would be a wiser and certainly softer choice for translation of "submission" into English. My wife has the edge in some areas, while I take responsibility in others; and that role changes over the years, depending on our gifts and growth. There is always a logical order of authority in any productive teamwork, which Hebraically is rarely cast in concrete, and teamwork is the name of the game.

But of even more significance, much of Paul's writings involved considerable problem solving in novice Gentile assemblies of formerly pagan mentality (read: legalists). As well as being a tad light on Hebraic insights, these groups often tripped over their latent pagan legalism. It doesn't mean that Paul's principles were pick-and-choose, but rather easily misunderstood by those who were not on the scene (see 2 Pet. 3:15-16). Moreover, hearing whispers from the Spirit of Abba was hardly a Hellenist norm!

So we wind it up. Perhaps the most wilted roses of all are today's parading protesters with feminist slogans and a hate-the-man mentality. Their most prominent rosy petals have fallen to the ground, trodden underfoot by the rest of humanity, and thorns are the fading identity of who they once had been. If they could only know who they were—and still are—on Abba's scale of values, they'd get in touch with their Divine Designer before the sun goes down.

Yet there are also those less than reliable lads, created to be a protective covering over the King's finest design for continuity of life. Whoever heard of a security guard defacing the priceless paintings in the art gallery he has been assigned to protect, or bashing up the V.I.P. placed under his authority for prime protection? Looks like too many of the guys inherited their manners from a macho Greek gymnasium mentality, where their mentors stripped them emotionally and morally from far more than their underwear!

The globe has gone mad. Old Snake Eyes with the help of the Hellenists has led humanity down a garden path, and we don't see the kings of the earth—or the United Nations above all—having either the wisdom or the will to fix it! If there ever was a time for the King of the Jews to show up, it's now. What say we hang in there strong until He makes it back?

ENDNOTES

1. To respond, my daughter and son-in-law have since initiated an orphanage for just such kids, along with a full program of related ministry in the hopelessly impoverished Para state of northeastern Brazil.

2. http://www.unhchr.ch/html/menu3/b/k2crc.htm.

3. For authentic videos of Palestinian terror training to children, check Middle East Media Research Institute on www.memri.org/video for stark translations from Arabic, www.honestreporting.com/relentless for their audiovisual, *Relentless* or info@spim.org.au for *Seeds of Hatred*. A broad range of other materials are also available.

4. An insightful Hebrew root for "train up" includes the concept of "dedication of his course," which beyond routine teaching, involves a covenantal commitment to Abba and with Abba for the child.

CHAPTER TEN

To Be Politically Correct or Die Trying

IN 2005, one of the major Australian Pro Basketball teams discovered the existence—not to mention the potential—of a 7-foot 7-inch (that's a shade over 2.31 meters) basketball center from somewhere in the U.S. and promptly signed him up for his talents. Come to think of it, his talents weren't even mentioned, only his size!

So that report led me to meditate on the accuracy of the politically correct fanfare in other matters of human rights, and in this case, the highly polished icon of equal opportunities.

Now, equal opportunities appear to be more important these days than more mundane matters such as truth and consequences. I think most of you have discovered by now that the media is a tad heavy on such issues as politically correct equality, while being a mite light on trivialities like truthfulness, for instance!

The problem is, equal opportunities for what? Take our well proportioned—for basketball anyway—rookie center noted above. I always wanted to be on our high school basketball team but compared with our new Aussie import, I was 2 feet short of stardom. So I had to carry the water jug (those were the days!) out to give a drink to the real heroes who were 5-foot-10 and upward. Where was my equal opportunity?

For thinking people, Psalm 139 compares to media mentality like an art gallery matches a scribble pad: *"For You created my inmost being; You knit me together in my mother's womb. I praise You because I am fearfully and wonderfully made; Your works are wonderful.... My frame was not hidden from You when I was made in the secret place. ...Your eyes saw my unformed body. All the days ordained for me were written in Your book before one of them came to be..."* (Ps. 139:13-16).

My experience with Abba tells me that I was chosen, designed, and born for a specific purpose to fit into the Creator's sovereign plans for a kid too short to play basketball. And my opportunity was to be what the Designer designed. And if we follow the Maker's manual, life makes sense. Otherwise, there's a lot of disappointment out there.

So does that mean I am against equal opportunities? Hardly!

When equality means no discrimination against race, gender, or social status, that concept mirrors exactly the moral justice of a righteous God whose divine standards delivered through Moses declare, *"Do not take advantage of a hired man who is poor and needy, whether he is a brother Israelite or an alien living in one of your towns"* (Deut. 24:14); and again, *"Do not deprive the alien or the fatherless of justice, or take the cloak of the widow as a pledge"* (Deut. 24:17; see also verses 15-16,18-22; and in the New Covenant, a parallel expression of fair treatment in James 2:1-19). His character traits of human equality are echoed throughout the Scriptures. We are born with imprints of life that are God given, and as such are covered by His compassion without partiality.

But by marked contrast, we must be very much awake to the subtle, politically correct fine print of the humanist agenda of the age. If humanistic appraisals in life are blind to earned qualifications, respectability, honesty, integrity, or moral decency, to pay no heed to personal performance for the sake of the rubber stamp of political correctness is stupidity at best and treachery at worst. Rather, any society that would hope to be blessed with any length of existence must recognize how each member can credibly use the imprints of life that God has given him. It has not an iota to do with an artificial politically presumed equality, manufactured by some-one's anti-God mentality.

So let us not confuse the Almighty's concept of divine justice with the wannabe merchants of greed, jealousy, competition, and covetousness in the name of equal opportunities. In the wisdom of the Most High, these non-virtues are not exactly His favorite attrib-utes. Therefore, acceptance of *who I am* has a guaranteed coverage by the divine justice of Almighty God. Dissatisfaction with *who I am* is uncovered by His judgment. And regardless of the much-touted, humanistic tool of political correctness, never the twain shall meet. *"Woe to him who quarrels with his Maker.... Does the clay say to the pot-ter, 'What are you making?'..."* (Isa. 45:9).

So what's a good summary of my beef with political correctness? Under the microscope, half of it feigns merit in being sensitive to the suffering of our fellowman. But it is the other half that flies defi-antly into the face of a sovereign Creator. That half seeks to regard our Maker's moral code as leftovers from yesterday's soup, substi-tuting some sort of *Political Correctness Manual* to line up the lem-ming-like puppets for a New World Order.

Guess what! My thesaurus programmed by up-to-date political-ly correct computer brilliance, presents *no equivalents* for "human-ism," "humanist," "humanistic," "demonic," "diabolic," "satanic," and a host of other anti-God descriptives. A moment of truth is that the subtle mind-manipulators of our day have infiltrated every avenue imaginable to deny that either they or their subversive thought-con-trol agenda even exist. Mind-boggling and chilling as well!

Excuse me a moment, I think it's Mrs. Adam's of Garden Grove on the phone again saying something about trying to be like God!

Now, this next issue coming up out of the *PC Manual* is ultra sensitive. In fact, it is so sensitive that in 1948 the United Nations gave it a massive amount of special attention in the Convention on the Prevention and Punishment of the Crime of Genocide, December 9, 1948.

"Genocide," according to the *Houghton Mifflin Company Dictionary*, means: "The systematic and planned extermination of an entire national, racial, political, or ethnic group." And the United Nations Convention on the matter adds a bit more to include, "mental harm to members of the group" (e.g. anti-Semitism which has *again* reached plague proportions in Europe), "killing members of the group," or "inflicting on the group conditions of life calculated to bring about its physical destruction in whole or in part" (e.g. suicide bombing of Israel's busses, restaurants, or city malls).

And we all agree—well most of us! But we'll get to that.

Like all good *PC Handbook* intentions—or inventions—there are a few hiccups. Let's start with the Bible. Let's have a look at a judgment system that the Almighty has reserved for Himself.

In the time of Noah, *"The Lord saw how great man's wickedness on the earth had become, and that every inclination of the thoughts of his heart was only evil all the time. The Lord was grieved that He had made man on the earth..."* (Gen. 6:5-6).

And so, He told Noah to build a floating zoo complete with keepers' quarters and then to get on board—you know the story. In fact, for benefit of the skeptics of our day, so has every primitive culture on the face of the earth known of that story to some degree!

Groups like the Wycliffe Bible Translators, along with a network of other Bible translation teams and worldwide Bible societies, have gone into jungle and rainforest depths to find myriads of remote tribal groups and tongues. And they have discovered that nearly every *one* of over 5,000 ancient tribal languages has had some legendary record of The Great Flood. Very interesting!

Well, that was a while back, and that big flood was something like what some call genocide. But that was the judgment of God, and either the savvy boys don't believe it at all, or else they like to look the other way. On the other hand, God (He had His reasons) did tell Moses on a couple of occasions, and Joshua, and King Saul as well, to "destroy everything that breathed." It would appear that most of the time they didn't actually carry it out, but regardless, that's why some people don't like the Bible. But I guess that's their problem of perception on how the sovereign Creator of the Universe ought to behave. It's amazing how highly polished some folks get these days!

But for the rest of us whose names are not Moses, Joshua, or Saul, *"Thou shalt not kill"* seems to be clear enough, and if you multiply that by 1,000 times, you come up with an identical thumbs down on genocide for any beginner who has never personally created his own galaxy!

And reflecting back on God's sovereignty over that massive toll of human life in the Indian Ocean Tsunami of 2004, if God is God, it had to be within His choice to cancel the "visitors visas" for some 200,000 souls He had granted permission to live on planet Earth for an unspecified time. It can be no other way. Anyone who knows Abba must eventually come to the conclusion that "coincidence" is not in His thesaurus. It's just like the words "humanism" and "satanic" aren't found in my thesaurus that, sorry to say, have been prepared by those with a NWO agenda.

Even the lawmakers and insurance adjustors call things like this an "act of God"; whether they actually believe it or not makes no difference. If it's in their contract, they have to pay. The bottom line is that humanity has forever and a day been trying to fix things over which they have totally no control and can only go so far. More Band-aids for those inevitable terminal appointments!

So back to man's mandate regarding genocide: What the United Nations really meant in the 1948 Convention was to prevent any repetition of the wanton, merciless, and inhuman annihilation of six million Jews from all across Europe from 1939 to 1945. We have already touched on this devastation as we began Chapter Eight looking at the issue of Human Rights, but the parallel issue of genocide now requires that we refer to it again. Sadly, those well-meaning intentions of an initially aroused UN have long fizzled out, and the Jew remains on the auction block as expendable to more important global issues from crude oil to even cruder Middle Eastern bigotry.

Thus the very race that the Convention on Genocide meant to protect is still very much in the firing line of human hatred. Some six decades on, the holy books that influence a massive majority of Islam still teach that the Jewish infidel must be destroyed—nor dare we forget their Christian targets either. Moreover, it is of less than small consolation that even the more moderate minds of Islam suggest that merely driving all Jews out of the Middle East might sufficiently sooth their collective nerves on this Jewish nuisance!

Meanwhile, the manufactured propaganda that presumes Arab ownership of Israel's ancient homeland is a political tsunami of another ilk. The "revision" of historical facts about who lived in the land from the 19th century onward, rolls on as a massive tidal wave of deception,[1] and the well-intentioned alarm bells of the 1948 Convention on Genocide have backlashed against the Jews like you wouldn't believe. In fact, the politically correct propaganda of the day is that the Jews' return to their ancient homeland was a gross failure, and that Israel has no business remaining in the Middle East.

But there are a few other facets to the United Nation's well-intentioned genocide-prevention farce, namely blatant hypocrisy. Reflecting back to when Yeshua "spoke with authority and not as the scribes," He made it clear that without doubt He regarded hypocrisy to be the most devious deed of all.[2] Genocide is but one sin—mass murder. Hypocrisy is two—mass murder, plus a pious look from atop the high moral ground. But never mind that political correctness puts "justified genocide" on another page altogether. Better days are on the way. The King of the Jews was not impressed with the hypocrisy of His day; neither is His Abba impressed with the hypocrisy of ours.

It would appear that—much like playing God—any qualifying superpower can legalize a license for "justified genocide" to destroy entire cities under the slogan of "saving lives in the long run." If you're big enough and rich enough to get away with it, you just do it. If you have a green light from the god of military muscle, who dare stop you? It once more brings to mind Lord Acton's wisdom: "Power corrupts and absolute power corrupts absolutely."[3]

But to understand the revised rules of genocide since World War II and the 1948 UN Convention on the Crime of Genocide, there is no better place to look than in the former Yugoslavia.

The scenario begins in 1992 in the former Serbian Bosnia-Herzegovina. NATO and Western friends jumped into the fray to flush out the Serb military leaders who had been charged with genocide against their lifelong Croatian enemies, as well as the even longer-term Islamic in-migrants. The Croatians had committed massive genocide against the Serbs as World War II was winding down, and the Serbs had some good reason to suspect that the hated Croats were about to pull it off again around the end of the '80s. So those quick-thinking Serbs committed some fairly serious atrocities against the Croats in a first-time payback so the Croats couldn't commit genocide the second time in a row against the Serbs. Get it? It's the Balkans, and not exactly new screenplay for that part of the world.

Now, had these been the only players in the game, it might have been resolved far more simply. But this time there was a difference. Remember those Muslims who had filtered into Serbia as immigrant laborers from Turkey some hundreds of years before? Over the years, they had built not a few mosques in the area, and every good Muslim knows that this now means that the land no longer belongs to the Serbs. Sadly, their gods had never passed this little change of ownership detail on to Belgrade, so a bit of trouble began to brew.

Now the peace-loving Muslims would never have thought of genocide had the Croats not brought it up. So this was their golden opportunity to side in with the Croats against the Serbs, who prayed to the wrong god anyway. Never mind that the Croats had no time for Allah either. When you've got the chance to wipe out those nasty Serbs, you might come up with some unusual bedfellows. Anyway, by that time, they figured it was long past the overdue date to let the Serbs know that the land no longer belonged to them, because they had built mosques to prove it! Hmm.

Of course, the world knew that it really was Serbia's fault all along because the media told them so. After all, when three nations are playing genocide-roulette, the one to do it last and who gets caught by NATO is in trouble. (I might have said the UN, but they never bother catching terrorists. They invite them in for tea, make them promise not to blow up more busses, and then nominate them for a Nobel Prize for peacemaking!)

Anyway, getting caught by NATO is different, especially if Islam is involved. The West has a few standing accounts with the Middle East, not only with an oil bill or two, but also to make them feel that the West isn't really that anti-Muslim after all. So this time, when Serbia lost out in the genocide triangle, they got their cities bombed by the West, and were made to cede ground to the Muslims. Since NATO doesn't bomb civilians all that often, they make good judges on who dares to commit genocide! Suffice it to say that an unbiased observer from Mars might readily conclude that any genocide that stabilizes the global price of oil must indeed be legitimate!

In 1999, Kosovo was a parallel replay of the same game, and as in any war, the civilian population bore the bloodshed yet again from Islamic land demands by former immigrants "proving" their right to the ancient Serb heartland. And the sturdy foundation stones of the NWO-to-be, once more gave the insurgents a helping hand for the cause of "world stability." So here's one to remember: The love of money is the root of all evil; but the love of oil is the root of all money!

And the identical scenario is once more being reprogrammed for Israel as I write. But the good news is that Israel has a few more end-of-days Bible prophecies published about it than does either Bosnia or Kosovo. So we take heart. And we watch, and we pray. And we remember the words of the One who promised to come back one day to see how we were making out: *"As it was in the days of Noah, so it will be at the coming of the Son of Man"* (Matt. 24:37).

Therefore, may we make our position very clear on all of this: War is a devastation that an all-too-human United Nations has been unable to stop. Genocide at the behest of human hands is an abomination to which, instead of curtailing, the UN unfortunately has opted to shut its eyes. Those nations who are large enough and strong enough to commit mayhem, murder, and genocide commit it with impunity—but of course with an excuse that they have a justifiable moral right to do it.

Moreover, in the myriad of skirmishes since World War II, despite the United Nations declarations to terminate these evils from genocide on up, Islam is always on hand to get another slice of the global pie (read: land grab) that the less powerful are always obliged to give up; the West keeps its pumps pumping profits; the developing world is preoccupied with survival; and in any case, the Judeo-Christian morality is irrelevant to the ongoing balancing act between Islam and the New World Order for their competing blueprint of One-World government.

On one hand, we have the ominous Islamist vision of global Shari'a Law, while on the other, the over-optimistic leaders of the so-called "Christian" West are more than preoccupied in funneling themselves into an economically dominating New World Order. Equipped with their *Politically Correct Handbook*, they are ready to rewrite their own laws, with latter-day insights on "good and evil"—or is it profit and loss? And like the arrow in the mega shopping mall tells the disoriented shopper, "you are here," we, indeed, are *there*!

And there's yet one more small life-and-death matter as we close this chapter. The god of these NWO folks has its genesis in global markets instead of Garden Management, and when they go, they're gone. The glitter of their day goes out for the long, long night, and as far as they know, that's their last chance to do business. But for me, and I think for you too, that Garden of God will eventually be coming back in all its original beauty and more. Slithering Sam will have gone out of business himself, and whether our own divine transfer is sooner or later, is not all that much of an issue.

It seems to be a minor detail to them because their *PC Manual* doesn't really have much to say about eternal life. But as a shabby second, they do have some revised philosophy on how to lengthen our current lifestyle for a few days. For example, if an armed bandit bursts onto your premises, or perhaps into a bank with a knife or a gun, give him what he asks for. Don't risk your life, for goodness sake. It's not worth it!

I agree. The paltry cash isn't worth it. But the undying principle of right and wrong is!

Gone are the heroes of principle, and principle itself is fading fast. Moreover, godly discipline in this encroaching age of well-oiled anarchy has now become a collector's item.

Who says it's not worth it to risk your life for truth? Or for principle? Or for *the* Truth? It's not worth it *only* if one presumes that this is all there is, and when you're gone, it's all over.

I was absorbed in an amazing inconsistency during the passing of Pope John Paul II. When he was so near death, that infamously infallible media was showing clip after clip of the mourners-to-be wringing their hands in anguish. "I fear the worst...I fear the worst." The worst? Lady, am I reading you right? The man is 84 years old, and if he is the hero you herald him to be, where are you coming from with this "worst" bit? Sadly, the media must have selected (again) those onlookers whose *PC Handbook* doesn't give them too much hope for tomorrow.

But for the faithful, the Scriptures are replete with, *"The righteous perish, and no one ponders it in his heart; devout men are taken away, and no one understands that the righteous are taken away to be spared from evil. Those who walk uprightly enter into peace; they find rest as they lie in death"* (Isa. 57:1-2). And then there is, **"Precious in the sight of the Lord is the death of His saints"** (Ps. 116:15; see also 2 Kings 22:20; John 5:24-27; Rev. 14:13; and a panorama of related biblical insights into quality life after death).

But their *Politically Correct Handbook* seems to have a far greater and grander agenda that doesn't concern itself with details like who might be the last one to turn out the lights!

ENDNOTES

1. *The Demise of Distorting History*, and *Who Occupies Whose Land?* under Articles on http://www.spim.org.au, or http://www.spim.org.au/articles/article3.doc, or http://www.spim.org.au/article4.htm. See Endnote 38.

2. For Jesus' exposé on hypocrisy within a segment of the Pharisaic teachers of the law in New Covenant times,

see Matthew 23:13-39. Although there is no single-word equivalent in Hebrew, the concept of pretense and deceit is berated throughout the *Tanakh*, particularly by Isaiah and other prophets. See Isaiah 58.

3. See The Phrase Finder on http://www.phrases.org. uk/meanings/288200.html.

CHAPTER ELEVEN

WITH POLITICAL CORRECTNESS WHO NEEDS AN ANTICHRIST?

THE publication date of my previous book, *Showdown of the Gods*, was bizarre. The manuscript surfaced on the publisher's desk exactly on September 11, 2001, ironically containing two tongue-in-cheek jibes about the World Trade Center, penned well in advance of that now infamous date. At one point I mused on, "...the nations becoming a bit edgy about getting their airliners or World Trade Centers blown up if they happen to pick the wrong side in an international dispute."[1] Then later on in the book, I made another prickly point on the naïve sense of U.S. security in places like devastated Oklahoma City or that earlier 1993 attempt on the World Trade Center, quipping that terrorist attacks in places like these are impossible because "...they are so far from the Middle East!"[2] And whammo, it happened again big-time on *the very day* of publication!

It was 2:00 A.M. in Cairns, Australia, an unlikely hour for one to wait up until the wheels of progress begin to roll in workday U.S. where my new book was imminently heading for the printers. I had just discovered two more last-minute typos to correct before the manuscript moved into that mode of no return, and I urgently wanted to contact my publisher.

A decidedly distraught editor answered the phone. She just happened to be the one who had initially processed and approved my manuscripts. Even for a tropical Queensland Australian night, the conversation that ensued was a not a little chilling.

"Did you hear the news?" she panicked. Now, at 2:00 A.M., I am not customarily watching the news, and I replied accordingly. Her desperation flowed on, "...this plane went into that tower and that plane went into this tower..." Look, I didn't even know what the architecture of the WTC looked like—only what the place was for. She lost me blind on whatever towers she was talking about until I heard, "...Pentagon..." and I was finally orbited into reality. "...and there's one plane still up there; we don't know where it's headed. We're under attack!"

Then there was that mini-eternity of several seconds of stunned silence. In those wee hours of the morning, it usually takes me a tad longer than normal to process moments of truth. She eventually came back with, "Are you surprised?"

I was unprepared for the announcement, but not totally surprised. I knew that Osama bin Loaded-up had been trying—and still is for that matter—to inject a suitcase nuke or nukes into his vitriolic assessment of America's sins, but the suicide hijack thing was a bizarre twist to any research files. "No," I replied; and taking into account my mixed insights above, "You're the one who proofread my manuscript!" Most of us with an eye on the Hebrew prophets, a nose for news, and an ear to the ground knew similar things were—and still are—coming.

Needless to say, 10:00 A.M. on 9-11 in the U.S. was not the best time to discuss correcting mundane matters like two typographical errors! So I made off to bed for a few hours, rose reasonably early, and called my good editor again in her afternoon. The fourth aircraft had by then crashed in Pennsylvania. Fortunately, there were no others, and the initial haze of turning that devastating corner that forever jarred the world's complacency, was beginning to clear. The two spelling errors in my manuscript received due attention by

4:00 P.M. Central U.S.A. time. But in the interim, a new era of global terror had been clandestinely launched.

And a new insight into biblical prophecy was unearthed. In Showdown of the Gods, I had detailed technical evidence for at least the beginning of events that had been prophesied for five of those last seven trumpet blasts of Revelation renown.[3] And I even suggested a possible Temple Mount scenario for Trumpet Number Six.[4] But I missed the venue completely. It fell upon Mohamad Atta to commandeer that devastating opener in New York instead of Jerusalem!

I often quip in my seminar lectures that 40 years ago I knew everything there was to know about end-of-days prophecy. Then, 30 years ago I started over!

At the moment I am sure of two things. The first one is that on the morning of September 11, 2001, the Sixth Trumpet of end-of-days prophecy had unmasked the horrendous face of that dreadful army of 200 million terrorists, (the Islamist-soft media like to ease them off as "militants") who had been foreseen to emerge from the environs of the Euphrates River. *"...Release the four angels who are bound at the great river Euphrates...kept ready for this very hour and day and month and year...to kill a third of mankind. The number of the mounted troops was two hundred million. I heard their number"* (Rev. 9:14-16; note also verse 13). This, of course, was not the prophecy completed, but the prophecy begun.

Peaceful Islam? It would indeed be welcomed, but with upwards of 1,200 million adherents of Islam spanning the globe at this writing, it would take a mere one out of six less than peaceful Islamists to be involved in some channel of global terrorism, to make up the 200 million of those predicted troops who are to traumatize their targets.

Strategists for the terrorists hold key positions in every major university of the globe; to stealthily rewrite history, they are on every tertiary textbook and encyclopedia revision committee. They hold unsettling lobbies in upward of 80 percent of every global government, not to mention an overwhelming influence in the United Nations, from a massive majority in the General Assembly to every one of its strategically rooted worldwide committees. And above all, they have over the last two decades, secured an inordinate leverage of leftist support from an anti-God-of-the-Bible worldwide media.

Moreover, in an incredible irony, they have no address. No one government has to fund them, yet they have an abundance of support from faceless entities of universal obscurity. They will buy their own bread and hire their own bed just for the privilege of massacring Jew and Gentile infidels, or anyone else who happens to get between them and their intended Judeo-Christian victims.

Think it through. Despite all the "good Islam" of which we have been advised, only 17 percent of their entire number is actually required for that predicted legion of 200 million terrorists, which of course, includes the logistic and financial support of those who supply terrorists, strategize for them, or cover up for their whereabouts. But by yet another disturbing measurement, repeated polls throughout the Middle East "moderates" who are supposed to hopefully "tolerate" infidels, from 60 to 80 percent avow that *world peace can only* **come when Israel is destroyed as a nation**, *and terrorism is the only way to get the noble deed done.* Go figure!

But irony of ironies, these self-styled executioners get some of their most wacky assistance from the "democratic" shackles so highly venerated by the very people they seek to destroy. Since the lion's share of all of today's terrorism is carried out by a specific age group, from a proven ideological background, and from a statistically glaring ethnic segment of society, to disregard that data for the protection of the life and limb of the innocent is no less than the suicide game that these perverted people are prone to play.

But in most Western nations—and especially in the U.S.A.— "profiling" for these dropouts from human sanity is a "violation" of that sacred cow of human rights, and Old Betsy begins to bellow like you wouldn't believe. The West has been lured into swallowing that cyanide capsule of political correctness, and Betsy now dutifully provides the children with the milk of demonic deception. I think we've also seen this movie before!

So much for terrorism. Fried blood in the subways, charred remains in the ashes of an airliner, or bits of human flesh plastered on walls 100 meters away from ground zero—any ground zero—need little additional amplification.

But do monitor the papers and watch the news. Beyond the happenings of the hour, pay special heed to the global media's jaded version of truth as they present their own interpretation, and you can knock off two pigeons with one pebble. You can both pick up what's happening globally, and with a tad of talent, you can soon begin to detect how a leftist media hopes you will gulp down their take on it. And your best media reality check possible is to run it through the filter of the biblical prophets. You can't miss.

Now you will recall that I mentioned that there are two moments of truth for end-of-days biblical prophecy that I am confident to identify with certainty; and I have just uncovered and presented the first one from the Sixth Trumpet blast of Revelation. The second one, seemingly far more benign than burned flesh or spattered blood, is a present-day exposé of those mind-benders of Hellenistic origins. But because it has become so much a part of our lives, our society, and the Western culture that we literally breathe, this assault upon our well-being must certainly be far more lethal than bombs that intermittently traumatize the public at large. Up to now at least, bombs end up killing relatively few in proportion to the publicity and the fear they produce.

The other hidden prophetic imagery that for some years now has been paraded before our very eyes—and I should include ears—has involved that nefarious beast that is to surface from the sea in chapter 13 of Revelation. We'll get to this cryptic creature himself in the next chapter, but for the moment, one specifically mentioned feature of this ferocious monster is his mouth:

"The beast was given a mouth to utter proud words and blasphemies and to exercise his authority for forty-two months. He opened his mouth to blaspheme God and to slander His name and His dwelling place and those who live in heaven.

He was given power to make war against the saints and to conquer them. And he was given authority over every tribe, people, language and nation" (Revelation 13:5-7).

If there is anything in the entire universe that gives us an illuminating picture of the present-day global media, my friends, this is it! Read through the above text one more time—slowly and comparatively with what that "mouth" is slated to do and say.

Twenty years ago, I would have told you *exactly* what those 42 months stood for, but not now. Sure I know the symbolism—like half of seven years—but there's a lot more behind it than that. There has been so much phony prophetic presumption put out that not only doesn't happen, but that also puts blinders on seekers who never will see. Moreover, I don't see that it would add any significance to the point we are making here.

The real happenings of the end of days are indeed proceeding right under our noses, but so many of the saints have been so pre-programmed with bad guesses including timing, that they can't even smell what's going on, let alone see it! Thus, I have been moved to identify only what we can see with utmost accuracy at this point of time, and leave the remaining guesswork to those prophecy buffs who have refused to recheck Scripture on what they already "knew" 40 years ago!

So for sure, we can focus on those two realities: The Sixth Trumpet was blown on 9-11, beginning a flow-on of global terror; and the second is the mouth of that beast most dreadful (compare also Dan. 7:7), which is no more and no less than a massive unassailable method of media reeducation. It is a system that possesses worldwide power, authority, and control like no other human entity could have ever even dreamed of in eons past. Nor could they have envisioned its influence, as it spreads a subtle but sure anti-Christ message like a tsunami of tsunamis. Who can argue with a computerized message? Who can challenge a myriad of far-off and unassailable microphones, or who can correct the record and set straight the universal cacophony of deceit? There is but One, and we pray that His intervention will be soon.

Let's have a closer look behind these convincing voices, the captivating calls from the electronic visitations into our living rooms, or in the print media—the authoritative newspaper reports that seem so routinely dependable lying there on the office desk or kitchen table.

First off, the electronic newscasts are bad enough. Almost all—and certainly all the major players—have their own unwritten anti-God agenda, which is a filter through which *all* reports must pass. Pocket-sized Israel is horribly maligned throughout the news networks in any and all of their serious attempts of defense against the violence from among their near neighbors. This bias is hardly because their politicians are so sanctified, but because their Creator God who has His own fascination with the future of Israel is. Nor is this even to mention the immeasurable local media influence from the 22 Arab nations that surround Israel's outer perimeter. Many of these, who in across-the-board revulsion of those sons of Jacob, even serve to goad Israel's violent nearer neighbors on to the boiling point.

In an irony of ironies, Fox News Network has been lauded by most Bible-believing Christians as the only commercial television network in the U.S.A. that they could trust, for honesty in reporting, for generally conservative views, and in particular, for an even-handed approach in reporting matters that concern Israel.

So guess what! In September 2005, it was reported by the *Gulf Daily News* that a Saudi Arabian Prince bought 5.46 percent of Fox's shares. In my first draft of this chapter, I penned pessimistically, "If your most reliable news channel has gone a bit negative on Israel by the time we go to print, you may have a good idea why. The noose tightens." And tighten it did, even before we got to press!

In an eleventh-hour editing of my manuscript, I am now able to include the sequel entitled: "Fox News Schooled by Saudi Prince." And the report goes on to say:

Billionaire Saudi Prince al-Walid bin Talal on Monday told the Arab and World Media Conference in Dubai that during last month's street protests in France that he put in a phone call to America's FOX News network after he disapproved of their reports that the rioters were Muslim-backed. Prince Talal, a major shareholder of the conservative television news channel, stated that within 30 minutes of his call, "Muslim riots" were changed to "civil riots."[5]

Almost everyone I talk to actually acknowledges that the media totally misrepresents reality, but the hitch is that ordinary people do not have a handle on the research or the financial resources that would catch them red-handed. I have a file full of malicious anti-Israel reports that could push this book up to 50 chapters. This, of course, would give neither one of us all that much joy, so I will limit it to one classic incident. But to get the full impact of print media sleight of hand, I strongly urge you to search for yourself in the *Honest Reporting* archives as well.

On September 30, 2000, the *New York Times* along with the *Associated Press* and other major media outlets published a front-page photo report on Tuvia Grossman, a Chicago-born Jewish student who was newly visiting Israel. He and two friends were in a taxi in a Jerusalem suburb heading to pray at the time-honored and highly revered Western Wall—a place of sanctity for both Jews and Christians. En route he was dragged out of the taxi and ruthlessly attacked by a Palestinian mob, brutally beaten, and stabbed. Grossman managed to escape to a nearby Israeli police post, when a media photographer snapped a photo of the ensuing melee. Grossman was central in the photo that shows blood pouring out from his head and soaking into his shirt collar. Behind him in the picture was an Israeli policeman with a baton raised toward the attackers who would have been in the forefront of the scene, but not close enough to Grossman to be caught in the photo. And the *Times/AP* caption for the photo? "Israeli Policeman and a Palestinian on the Temple Mount"—with the obvious cynical insinuation that a vicious Israeli policeman was beating a poor defenseless Palestinian who turned out, in fact, to be an overseas Jewish student and a victim *of* the Palestinians and hardly of the policeman who was rescuing him![6]

This type of worldwide anti-Semitic media bias is invariably slanted against Israel and her people. And even when caught out, corrections are rare and apologies even more like molars on an amoeba.[7]

Another statistical study by *Honest Reporting* on headings in London-based Reuters—again in slurring Israel—shows incontrovertible bias. In violent acts against Israelis, the Palestinian agent is named in only 33 percent of their headlines. But in violent acts against any Palestinian—regardless of what they did to provoke the action—the agent (generally Israel) is named in 100 percent of their headings. In the same study, regarding *Reuters'* verb usage in their report titles—in violent acts effected by the Palestinians, only one third are put into the active voice, thereby "softening" the maliciousness of the deed. But if an Israeli—most often in the case of defensive measures—initiated the violence, 100 percent of the titles are in the active voice with an effect of magnifying the "aggression."[8]

This can be statistically measured not only with *Reuters* coverage, but also if other news sources are analyzed, similar bias patterns can be found as well. This might register a "so what?" to the indifferent observer, but linguists and journalists well know the spin that can be put on any report. But it is hardly limited to the print media. If you listen carefully to the nightly news, it shouldn't take a Ph.D. in fudge-making to tell who is the target and who is on the *proteksia* side of the bulletin. Excuse me, is it supposed to be news or network preferential spin? (Read: anti-Semitic propaganda.)

Due to the direction and involvement of my ministry over the years, my fattest files in these biased media agendas happen to deal with anti-Semitism and the Jews who—with ample practice ever since the days of Pharaoh—seem to have somehow learned to live with it.

But now, let us turn our attention to other innumerable parallels of media-sourced political correctness for the process of "reeducating" the masses. The naïve and unsuspecting public must be turned away from any and all suggestion of those archaic bedrock biblical values. Despite the media manipulation for the myriad of well-oiled Middle Eastern priorities, from global terror to global trade, there are a multitude of other voices of Hellenistic fervor in the queue to lobby for their own lion's share of free publicity in the press. All lined up for their free lunch in the broadcasters' banquet hall, their messages of newfound freedom, fun, and frolic are ready to flow.

In the TV sitcoms, shows like "Everybody Loves Raymond," "The Simpsons," and a host of others are hilarious amusement to the crowd who loves to see the Abba-designed family structure belittled, degraded, and ripped to shreds like rotten rags. The father figure, who God has ordained to family defense and covering, comes off as a sheer simpleton to be pitied; the mother is generally the sharper one while the younger set are a pack of razorblades. Those are but two examples from volumes of politically correct reprogramming away from a Hebraic-ordered value system.

But does it ever occur to the mini-minded multitudes that even though school kids have learned to conquer cyberspace with a computer they have neither designed nor programmed, it has nothing to do with their wisdom, maturity, or capacity to develop meaningful and enduring relationships? Back to our opening focus in Chapter Nine—does no one wonder why the street kids, who have no home and no known father to answer to, are popping up in endemic proportions like worldwide mushrooms? Of course, sidesplitting sitcoms are far cooler teaching techniques for a godless, New World Order mentality than boring textbooks. And teach they do!

And then, there are talk shows that generally reflect more politically correct parrots than serious reality. Islam is rescued from a clichéd cop-out called Islamophobia as the designer-cult of choice, while Bible oriented Judeo-Christian values are blatantly blasphemed. It's not that the glitter gals with telly-talents are headed all that fast to switch to a *burqa*, but it's in their PC agendas to get as many other fans as possible to follow the "faithful."

This is hardly to denigrate the convictions of modesty of Islam—far from it—but to expose the TV political pressures from the dentures of the beast all the way down to his tonsils. Regardless, Islamophobia is much more than a misnomer anyway, it's misspelled; it's Islamo-*bomber*phobia. The Scriptures I read, speak of the dignity of my fellowman, whether Muslim, Maoist, or Kentucky Moonshiner. I may not invest in their insights or buy into their business, but all are created in the image of God. But this is hardly to say that respecting a person means an equal esteem for his deeds, be it an idolatrous religious system or a cult perversion, such as the immoral practices in the gymnasiums of ancient Greece or even from more ancient Sodom. Give us a break, please!

But who or what conspiracy is behind all this? Perhaps we should ask the Garden guest of Mrs. Adam's? Sammy should surely know!

Much in the newspaper cartoon strips is more of the same. The "funnies" are less than funny. They serve as another overt caricature on deteriorating family values where less than brilliant jibes are a subtle stand-in for wisdom. Nonconformity is in, while principle, morality, and answering to a higher spiritual plane goes out with the empty coke bottles into the recycle bin. These are but another battery of the new teachers of a humanist age. And their salaries are indirectly paid by a sick society that is drawn to the minty flavor of their carefree messages.

So it goes until the 9-11's and the Katrinas and the tsunamis roll in, causing the freedom-mad New World orgy to pause dutifully for a moment of silence, and then with that detail accomplished, they once more roll on.

Moreover, the catchy classrooms of the neo-academic lecturers of learning are legion. We are inundated with all the politically correct currents throughout the film producers, and an overflow of reruns in videos. We are bombarded with the further echo of humanistic themes in music, and certainly not the least, the

Internet. These are now our new schoolmasters of reeducation from the stodgy Hebraic values of yesteryear.

Popularity polls have become the index in the *New Revised PC Bible*, to test the flow of whoever you know, in order to hide from view our universal insecurity among the popular opinion of the masses. And speaking of polls, in order to get the best political results out of once noble democracy—now mutating to mediocrity—one no longer needs to elect a giant of wisdom and strategy, but a charismatic charmer who has the glitz to patronize the polls in order to keep on top of the pile. No more Abe Lincolns, Gandhis, or Churchills, but far more clever fellows who can interpret "what the people want." (Compare the scenarios in 1 Samuel 8:6-7 and 1 Samuel 15:24-26.) Not surprisingly, what the people want is strangely similar to what the mouth of the beast—that colossal message of a politically correct global media—is subtly murmuring to every captivated puppet in the show.

But is this really what they want? Is it what you want? Yet this is what the politicos of the New World Order are building themselves upon, and where the end-of-days flow is sure to go. Wake up, Australia; wake up, America; wake up, Europe; wake up, world!

You know what? Those on our globe who resent a caring Abba poking His nose into their own private affairs have a shock coming with the political sharpies who are gearing up to control the NWO. First and foremost, it takes a lot of big bucks and political shenanigans to get to the top, and none of them got to be jillionaires because they were so benevolent to poor folks. Nor did they get up there because they were so honest. Those who reckon that Abba is so far from their self-centered sobbing for whatever they want now, have a monumental moment of truth in the offing!

It would seem that Slippery Sam of Garden infamy has a hand— no, not a hand but a coil—in this. Did you know that Sam is not a cobra to kill you quick? He's a python, who in due time, crushes the life from his clients who attend his classes to learn for themselves how to distinguish the difference between good and evil. We've said it twice before, but we must repeat it once more: *"Woe to those who call evil good and good evil, who put darkness for light and light for darkness, who put bitter for sweet and sweet for bitter"* (Isa. 5:20).

So with the mouth of the beast bombarding us with his own garden path insights by day and his lullabies by night—with an incredible tutor like that, who needs an antichrist?

And one last tip for you is to steer well clear of the mouth of the beast—he's got bad breath!

ENDNOTES

1. Victor Schlatter, *Showdown of the Gods* (Mobile, AL: Evergreen Press, 2001), 18.

2. Ibid., 146.

3. Ibid., Chapter 5, "Trumpets So Loud We Can't Hear Them"; and Chapter 6, "The Pit and the Pandemonium."

4. Ibid., 83.

5. ICEJ News and Analysis, Jerusalem, Israel, December 8, 2005.

6. For extremely valuable backup research see: http://www.honestreporting.com/articles/45884734/reports/The_Photo_that_Started_it_All.asp.

7. *New York Times*, in this case, did run a less than sincere correction after a major write-in initiated by Grossman's father, a Chicago doctor. A Paris court ordered the AP and one French newspaper to pay limited damages to Grossman that, of course, reflected more court order than admission of error. See full report: http://www.honestreporting.com/articles/45884734/reports/The_Photo_that_Started_it_All.asp.

8. See a full report of the study including a variety of actual examples. http://www.honestreporting.com/articles/critiques/Study_Reuters_Headlines.asp.

CHAPTER TWELVE

BEASTS AND ANTICHRISTS—
PROPHETS AND PROFITS

WE are now headed for a fascinating finale.

In these three final chapters, we're going to take a relatively new peek at a number of end-of-day concepts like the two beasts of Revelation 13, the red-robed prostitute of Revelation 17, and the complete demise of a much more than Islamic Babylon in Revelation 18. And we'll have a brief glimpse of 666—that number of guesses galore—as well as the scrutiny of an almost idolized antichrist that has been getting an inordinate amount of attention in the light of which prophecy-whiz can spot him first. This game of being the first one to tag the antichrist, we shall see, may be more like missing the forest for the trees than like figuring out which tree is named satan!

But first we've got to set a few things straight that aren't.

Millions of American Bible believers, including a few from Europe, Australia, and elsewhere are planning on getting out of here before bad things start to break forth. Well, looking at the worldwide news (I told you to watch the news, didn't I?), it looks like they might have already missed their bus. Not really. The good news is that it hasn't come yet.

The reason they thought that the rest of the road would be lined with roses is premised on two major errors. One is that they have been taught from the days of knickers until now a theory that is built on a locked-in "tribulation" period of seven years. Anybody who can count can figure out that it's been more than seven years since the stoning of Stephen, the martyrdom of the early Church, along with the slaughter of God-fearing Jews throughout the ages. And in our day, as well as for several decades now, there has been the butchering of multimillions of Christians in Africa, Indonesia, and elsewhere, plus "red flags" like 9-11, the London subways, the train massacre in Spain, the tsunamis, the Katrinas, and the Most High knows-what-else by the time you read this.

My Bible clearly reflects that no one will go anywhere *gracefully*—except via the cemetery—*until* Yeshua's feet once more touch the Mount of Olives, gathering to Himself the redeemed of the ages, as well as those God-fearing among His own people who—much like forward-looking Moses and David—have yet to visualize the totality of the promise. And if 16 of the Hebraic prophets are to be believed, *it will include* delivering a less than appreciated Judeo-Christian remnant from the venom of the nations (see Zech. 14:2-16).

Check it out. Yeshua told us to expect tribulation and to be on guard against all manner of attacks for our own good, but never to watch for it as a milestone in the end-of-days scenario. We're supposed to be *watching for Him*. So someone got it a bit mixed up. I have already written a well-documented chapter in my previous book on *what* versus *whom* we should be watching for and need not elaborate more on it here.[1]

And one other hiccup by the well-meaning armchair prophets of the 19th and 20th centuries was based on the *isolation* of one single verse from Paul's letter to the Thessalonians,

> *"For the Lord Himself will come down from heaven, with a loud command, with the voice of the archangel and with the trumpet call of God, and the dead in Christ will rise first. After that, we who are still alive and are left will be*

caught up together with them in the clouds to meet the Lord in the air. And so we will be with the Lord forever" (1 Thess. 4:16-17).

Now, this says it well, but it doesn't say it *all*. (Actually, the theory in question was first traced back to have originated with the Jesuits from the 16th century who may not have been the aces in biblical cross-references that one might have expected them to be!)

Sadly, our latter-day seers failed to note that the above verse from Thessalonians does not give either the *venue* or the *timing* of the "rapture"—as it is commonly called—and in their enthusiasm proceeded with a bit of their own theory to fill in those blanks. Unfortunately, their guesses were a bit off. Both the *location* of His return and the *sequence of preceding* events are spelled out in one or more of at least six other cross-references throughout Scripture referring to the identical happening—the return of the King of the Jews. Old icons of misunderstanding never die—they just get republished! But again, this is well documented in *Showdown of the Gods* with chapters and verses—all of them—for any and all who would like to search them out.[2]

Suffice it to say that the prophet Daniel never linked his cryptic "70th week" (see Dan. 9:27) with a presumed seven-year yardstick of tribulation, nor did Yeshua, nor did any other prophet. Both Daniel and Yeshua spoke of terrible trouble in the end of days, but neither ever suggested measuring its duration, nor even slicing it into salami cuts called *Pree, Mydd,* and *Poste.* This idea came from the Jesuits and from later 19th-century sages who sold it to the church, and the 20th-century "prophets" took it and ran. And unfortunately, much of the church never looked back—to the Scriptures that is, that might have cleared up the issue.

Yes, there is massive trouble even now. No, the Bible never says for how long, except "to the end," and yes, Yeshua is coming back to rescue His people. Now, let's get on to some equally intriguing matters, but hopefully less "super-sanctified" issues than who is going to get to fly first!

So let's have a look at a quickie—that captivating code of catastrophe, number 666 (see Rev. 13:18). Look, we've had nominations by the paperback prophets for this infamous figure, from bloodletting butchers to improbable princes. Let's give it a bit more serious scholarship than that, please.

What is humanism anyway? It is a humanity sold out to anti-God patterns in the triad of human components—body, mind, and spirit. It is a humanity imprisoned to physical passions of the flesh; it is a human entity embedded with a mind that is totally devoid of the Divine; it is a human spirit that is inseparably interlocked with the spirit of this age. In biblical insights, seven is the number of God, the number of completion. Six, however, is the number of man—an incomplete creature without his Abba. For those who presume the fantasy of reincarnation, unfulfilled humanity is headed for the recycle bin. For those among us who don't, unregenerate man has an even less favorable future!

True, there may well be some sort of a single head-honcho of the humanists at the close of the age. Throughout history there always has been a Nero Caesar, an Adolf Hitler, a Yasser Arafat, a prime entity of evil that elicited blood from his enemies.

Yet even more likely in these days of politically correct cosmopolitan control, a domineering antichrist-like authority could well be something of an international think tank like the CFR, the 4,000-member Council of Foreign Relations.[3] Based in the U.S., not a few analysts regard this body as the key planners for a New World Order. In fact, the far-reaching influences of this austere body may already be effecting their control far more widely than the unsuspecting flock of followers might imagine. Moreover, if you look up the footnote, you may be a bit surprised to find one or more of your favorite heroes on their membership list!

But why search for the antichrist as if he is some boogey man behind the bush, when his very agents flash you nightly with humanistic mind-bending message-movies right inside your own home? It's amazing how we prefer some fancy prophetic personality "out there somewhere" in an effort to keep the focus off our own backyard. Indeed, the human spirit much prefers to keep his back veranda swept clean of any and all antichrist insights that might get too personal for our own private lifestyles!

Throughout time and in an array of languages, even though "666" has most often been recorded as the whole number, six hundred sixty-six, graphically it can also carry an additional symbolic reflection of simply three sixes side by side. Let me suggest that it may merely reflect man—man—man; it is a classic representation of a humanity that has rejected their Abba's godliness and become humanistic in body, humanistic in mind, and humanistic in spirit. For cricket fans, scoring a 6 is not so bad. For sons of the Kingdom, it's not so good! Let's do a bit of revealing scriptural cross-comparisons.

We will note that these are the three and *only three* areas in which Yeshua was tempted: bread for the body, the promise of massive wealth for "peace of mind," and a sensational catch by angels to elevate the prestige of any flagging human spirit (see Matt. 4:1-11; Luke 4:1-13). They are repeated as the identical three areas we are commanded to commit to God in both the Torah—to love the Lord God with all our spirit-hearts, our soul-minds, and our body-strength—as well as repeat quotations of these three specific areas of human responsibility cited first in the Torah and then in at least three New Covenant references; see Deuteronomy 6:4-5; Matthew 22:37; Mark 12:29-30; Luke 10:27. And we also have one excellent additional commentary on these three key areas of human makeup in the first letter of John to his followers. *"For everything in the world—the* [body] *cravings of sinful man, the* [mind] *lust of his eyes, and the* [spirit] *boasting of what he has and does— comes not from the Father but from the world"* (1 John 2:16). An interesting observation is that John's antichrist discourse follows only two verses later!

Thus, the symbolism of 666 can serve to reflect a total rebellion in body, mind, and spirit against all three areas of Abba's designated authority. Not a bad candidate for the universal *"man of sin"*! So you can either be a representation of that perverted personality, or else a part of the Body of Messiah. But you can't be both. Thus, 666 stands quite clearly symbolic of that counterfeit body of the sin-man. But unfortunately, predicting the "antichrist" is far more intriguing than personal introspection!

Now, let us have a look at that beast of Revelation 13. Actually, there are two beasts that operate in tandem. This isn't all that hard. The primary one has seven heads and ten horns, has the direct sponsorship of satan, and comes up out of the sea. *"And I saw a beast coming out of the sea. He had ten horns and seven heads, with ten crowns on his horns, and on each a blasphemous name* (Rev. 13:1).

The second one has two little horns that make him look benign like a lamb, but his voice echoes otherwise. *"Then I saw another beast, coming out of the earth. He had two horns like a lamb, but he spoke like a dragon. He exercised all the authority of the first beast on his behalf, and made the earth and its inhabitants worship the first beast, whose fatal wound had been healed. And he performed great and miraculous signs, even causing fire to come down from heaven to earth in full view of men"* (Rev. 13:11-13).

Perhaps a well-meaning but missing-the-mark mentality in these matters has been twofold:

> 1) The temptation to be a sort of amateur armchair ana-lyst, able to assist those with inferior insights to under-stand before the time what these cryptic creatures might happen to be.

> 2) But above that, it has been presumed that their iden-tity is in the "who" category rather than the "what" cate-gory. There's quite a difference!

The latter assumption also contains the failure to recognize that biblical prophecy spans millennia and is repeated over and over and over again. Each repeat, of course, continues to point to the end of the age, for which everyone from the apostles through Martin Luther—to cite a beginning and a more midpoint example—were all hoping that they would still be around to see it.

So now, are we finally going to be a part of Messiah's return in the first decade of the 21st century? I for one would *like* to be and see possibilities, but in Kingdom reality, the jury is still out.

Now, this latter bit of info leads to one more problematic pitfall—trying to pin a nametag on these fearsome beasts of blasphemy to fit into our present scenario. We have had nominations for these creatures from Rome to Riyadh. We have had Protestants nominating popes and perhaps popes even returning the favor. We have had Hitler and a former U.S. Secretary of State named Henry what's-his-name; and even more recently a prince charming named Charlie whoever. It gets a bit embarrassing to even talk about some of these brilliant brainstorms.

So for a shortcut to reality, it may be far wiser to look at the "what" nature of these metaphoric monsters than the "who."

The first one comes from the sea, and has the direct sponsorship of satan—i.e., the dragon (see Rev. 13:2b, also Rev. 12:9). It has ten horns and seven heads.

In biblical symbolism, the sea represents the depths of wickedness, haunts of demonic forces, the playground for the satanic symbols of Leviathan and Rahab, and even the abode of the dead throughout a panorama of Scriptures. It also includes the Hebraic word *Sheol* that in some English versions is translated as "the depths," giving a fairly clear bio on the background of Beast number one.[4] Further association may be suggested in Luke 8:30-32, as well as the specific Hebraic imagery of Sheol and Leviathan in Job 38:16-17 and 41:1-34 respectively.

The seven heads appear to be geographical areas, or perhaps more accurately, nations or kingdoms. (For example, compare Revelation 17:9-11 in one such identity.) It could shock some of us who are a bit hung up on patriotism to a comfortably benevolent government, that *all* earthly gentile kingdoms are invariably grouped in a setting *against* the Kingdom of the Eternal One who is yet to come. And I doubt that this scriptural polarity will change all that much just because our favorite politician has a high regard for the Good Book and happens to get elected! Better make sure you get this one sorted out.

The prophet Daniel, on the other hand, didn't seem to get tied up so much on counting the nation-heads on the creatures he saw. In fact, he was frequently favored by the Ancient of Days in being personally given the divine interpretation that the beasts in his visions specifically represented certain nations of his time and even after. And, as history rolled on, the nations—that is, the Gentiles— were highly targeted in the proclamations by the Hebrew prophets. Once again, this is history's unique video of the Almighty's dealing with the nations of the globe who were fairly impressed with their own powers—for a while, that is!

So back to Revelation 13. Next to note are the ten horns. Horns represent power and plenty of it all the way from the symbolism of the all-significant altar of atonement (see Exod. 27:1-8) to live bulls, to other burly beasts, to all manner of less animated authority—like big bucks in our day, for instance.

Most interesting with regard to those ten horns, money is power (sort of like oil), and currently replacing the Most High for the god of the hour seems to be the global markets. With media blessings, their daily devotionals are offered at the end of every newscast. And on the high market holidays (read: market surges and recessions), the network might even throw in a whole half-hour of "prayer and praise" to this currently dominate deity, depending on whether the market is rising or falling. Look, friends, the beast is neither a bull nor a bear, but you're getting warm.

What is more, there are ten Western industrialized nations that dominate the International Monetary Fund by controlling the majority of votes, which may well give us another hint in this direction. Moreover, when you have the symbolism of *both* a horn and a crown, you have a combo of both a political and an economic entity. Therefore, it is worthy of note that we also have the G-7—the seven most industrialized nations, and of course the wealthiest[5]— that wield the big political stick over the "developing" nations. And of course, these are the ones with the fat bank balances to make it happen their way. Seven nationalistic heads, ten banking buddies? Hmm.

Of course, those 10–7 numbers have also surfaced in history past. It's impressive to note how the Ancient of Days has the capacity to come up with a 10–7 combo in almost every age to keep the pros of prophecy guessing in every changing scenario. Then there are those who have grown so weary of keeping an eye on Abba's most helpful biblical signposts, that they have even proposed that the entire prophecy slate be wiped clean with the first advent of Yeshua, and from now on, one must make his own way into the unknown. I might warn that this position takes not a few gallons of white-out per Bible to make the necessary corrections, but pros are pros, you know!

So to continue with this cryptic beast soon to surface, we've had different top dogs—dogs are beasts I reckon—from the days of King Nebuchadnezzar in Daniel's era to the present. But really, what difference does it make who happens to be at the top of the heap as the globe descends into the chaos of godless humanism now bursting its Hellenistic dikes? Therefore, whether the emerging New World Order is the *last gasp* of humanism before the King of the Jews comes back to do a table-overturning assessment on the global markets, I can't say for sure. But I would like to think that this might be so, since a lot of the pieces of the puzzle are now coming together.

But wait—there was another beast, wasn't there, who was as cute as Mary's little lamb but sang lullabies like Leviathan who we just met in the Book of Job? That was the one, *"coming out of the earth* [who] *had two horns like a lamb, but he spoke like a dragon"* (Rev. 13:11). Who's this fellow? Or what is it?

Let's check this out. Where did he come from? It was not the supernatural sea of wild demonic forces but *"out of the earth."* Remember who else came up out of the earth? If you are a bit new to these matters, his name was Adam, and his wife was Eve Adam's—Mrs. Adam's, that is. It's all there in Genesis Chapter 2.

Look, I don't think I should have to review much of this. There are two beasts in Revelation 13; one is of diabolical sources from the sea (otherwise known as Sheol—the domain of the dead), and the other represents the human sons of Adam. And this pair—the demonic and the man—seem to tango reasonably well together in the end of days. And to picture it just as simply as possible, the first beast—satan and cohorts—line up the program for the final rebellion against God, and the second beast—decadent humanity—puts legs on it and breathes life into its image. They create this antichrist combo in an effort to once and for all upstage the King of the Universe.

Obviously, any successful human insurgency that wants to be as clever—actually more clever—than God needs a highly qualified legion of tutors from Deep Sea Tech College along with a generation or two of highly competitive students willing to be well-grounded in the nitty-gritty of the New World Order. And the sum total of this beastly man of sin is 666, which—as we have seen above—is an earthen humanistic response in all three components of his makeup.

Mrs. Adam's, can you tell us who tutored you in getting your own program off the ground?

Let's go on. There are those among us who would make some of these things so complicated—so cryptic, so mysterious. I don't want to analyze their motives or even their mentality in the matter. On the other hand, did you know that the greatest blessings from Abba—including His insights—are free? And some of the greatest mysteries of life are ever so simple.

So next, what's with this antichrist fuss? First of all, don't honor him with a capital A. He's not worth it.

Ironically, this entire hubbub about a personified and fully accredited senior satan, comes from the second letter of Paul to the Thessalonians. We have already referred to his first letter earlier in the chapter in relation to another matter. But Paul had also written this second letter to these good folks in order to patch up one point they misunderstood in his first letter. Now this gets weird because we've got well-meaning folks today that continue to get sidetracked—all the way from then until now—in some of the same ruts that bogged the Thessalonians in their own end-of-days understanding. His second letter happens to include a warning that there will come a "man of sin" who will pervert the globe, even out-slithering Slippery Sam of Garden Genre. Let's see how Paul puts it:

> *Don't let anyone deceive you in any way, for that day will not come, until the rebellion occurs and the man of [sin] is revealed, the man doomed to destruction. He will oppose and will exalt himself over everything that is called God or is worshiped, so that he sets himself up in God's temple, proclaiming himself to be God. ... For the secret power of lawlessness is already at work; but the one who now holds it back will continue to do so till he is taken out of the way. And then the lawless one will be revealed, whom the Lord Jesus will overthrow with the breath of His mouth and destroy by the splendor of His coming. The coming of the lawless one will be in accordance with the work of satan displayed in all kinds of counterfeit miracles, signs and wonders, and in every sort of evil that deceives those who are perishing...*(2 Thessalonians 2:3-12 gives the full scenario).

So, you could flip a coin as to whether this *"man of sin"* is a sort of human Osama bin Caesar—or even some other NWO political personalities closer to home—or just plain humanistic lawlessness that engulfs us in a sea of evil environment.

From the text examination—exegesis we call it—it could go either way. Nevertheless, as I look around, I see that it wouldn't matter an iota who the top ogre may chance to be. Actually, what affects the believer more is the inescapable setting of a corrupt and decadent humanity. It's not necessarily the boss that bugs us, but the bottom line is that instability of rebellion and anarchy that is now beginning to daily swirl around us.

Nor does it matter either, what I see or what I think I see, but rather the necessity of matching this *"man of sin"* prophecy with cross-Scripture references. Unfortunately, not a few presume that Paul's terminology refers to some personified Antichrist with a capital A.

A mere 30 pages away from the Thessalonians text in my Bible—it could be a few pages more or less in your Bible—we have the only five references to *antichrist* in the entirety of Scripture, and this *"man of sin"* concept doesn't happen to be among them! All five references are found in the first general letter of John the apostle, and in his chapter 2, he clearly claims that, not *"an antichrist,"* but *"antichrists"* are already in an undisputed plurality. *"...as you have heard that the antichrist is coming, even now many **antichrists** have come. This is how we know it is the last hour"* (1 John 2:18, emphasis added).

Then he goes on in his fourth chapter to identify who *these guys* are—not who *this guy* is—namely full-blown humanists from the other side of the Great Divide (see 1 John 4:1-6). That gives very strong suggestion that Paul's *"man of sin"* reference represents, not a single human superman, but an immense *generational mind-set* of godlessness in an age of anarchy. Suffice it to say that *antichrist* is a theological anti-God position; the humanistic *man of sin* is the result.

Obviously, there will always be a human strongman available to lead, but *"setting himself up in the temple of God"* seems to have much more to do with trying to replace the Almighty's own sovereignty with today's humanistic substitutions, than it does with trying to invent some latter-day parallel to the Greek Antiochus Epiphanes' killing of a sacrificial pig on the Temple altar back in 168 B.C.!

Mrs. Adam's and Garden guest enlightened us how to play God—even without a physical temple—a few eons back, and the Hellenists have been helping polish our expertise ever since. Thus, I suggest we cease wasting our time taking "sanctified bets" on who the bit players may be that the deceiver will choose to use in his end-of-days strategies. Instead, may we focus on the *principles* under which the Master Potter has been plying the clay for generations until He makes His own final move. Figuring out prophecy isn't everything, but goofing it up isn't anything!

It is incredible how those two simple, straightforward letters to the Thessalonians each inherited end-of-days, add-on ideas that simply did not exist when Paul penned his Epistles. Thus, it's hard to say whether this is good news or bad news, but the news is that you won't have to wait one day more for that infamous antichrist to show up. We already have more of him around us than we know what to do with. Back to the big arrow on the info map in the mega-mall—you are here!

ENDNOTES

1. Victor Schlatter, *Showdown of the Gods* (Mobile, AL: Evergreen Press, 2001), Chapter 8.

2. Ibid., 103. Notice especially endnote 3.

3. See: http://www.answers.com/Council%20on%20Foreign%20Relations. The membership list makes interesting research.

4. A few of the multiplicity of texts that suggest linkage of the sea to sin, Sheol and the demonic are Exod.15:5-8; Isa. 51:9-10; 57:20; Ps. 69:14-15; 139:8-9; Dan. 7:2; Mic. 7:19; and Jude 13.

5. Russia is from time to time included in a G-8, but their financial limitations deny permanent status.

CHAPTER THIRTEEN

MULTIPLICATION OF MAMMON
FOR THE GREAT DIVIDE

THERE are some very bedrock basics from the teaching of the Son of Man, that far too many of us have forgotten for far too long, yet there's a verse from His Sermon on the Mount that sticks in the backside of my brain like glue. *"No one can serve two masters. Either he will hate the one and love the other, or he will be devoted to the one and despise the other. You cannot serve both God and Money"* (Matt. 6:24; also Luke 16:13).

In my old King James Bible, they called it "mammon." Not a bad word! Language changes, English changes, translations have changed to clear up a lot of archaic expressions. But "mammon" sticks. Perhaps that's the epoxy side of it that keeps it in my subconscious. On the other hand, mammon is more than money—much, much more.

The first half of the verse above, however, snaps the photo from another angle. You can't "serve two masters"—you can't go in two directions at the same time. I think that might be the simplest summary of this whole book. The Greek head-benders said you could play pendulum and get away with it. But the Abba of Abraham said, "No way," while the Mentor of Moses spelled it out without a loophole, "You shall have no other gods besides Me" (Exod. 20:3).

One of the most aggressive acts that the Gentle Teacher of Galilee ever came up with was recorded close to the beginning of the Gospel of John. John must have been overtly overawed at the outburst, because Matthew, Mark, and Luke all recorded the turning-of-the-tables incident much later in their Gospels, but John puts it up front. Yeshua charges through His Father's temple courts, dumps the tables of the moneychangers upside down, and mammon runs all over the stones and down the cracks (see John 2:13-17). A bit of a banker's meltdown, you might guess. Not exactly the way to make your debut if your ultimate agenda is to run for Chief Rabbi!

Was the Master making somewhat of a Free Market Economy statement? Or was it a pro-hermit pitch like going back to the Essene communities, or some nostalgic throwback to short-circuiting a cash economy by gathering manna only from the desert? Not quite. Let's see this thing clearly.

It was His initial singularity-of-life-purpose declaration of one master with no mammon mixed in. It was the Great Divide between the increasingly popular Greek mind-set of "this life is all there is, so buy into it now," versus His Abba's alternate vision of heading for a higher plane through intimacy with the King of the Universe. But don't cast off all your cash; you'll need some to pay taxes to Caesar, or to buy your own bread so you can share a bit of it with the hungry, or maybe even buy perfume to anoint the feet of the worthy—whatever. But don't you dare make your paltry profits off of my Papa's House of Prayer! *"I will not yield My glory to another"* (Isa. 48:11b), says the Creator of the Galaxies.

Yeshua also said heaps more about the pursuit of assets from pennies for the poor to investment portfolios that too many of us moderns have rationalized to the too-hard basket. He talks about treasures in Heaven, about trusting for tomorrow, about being cared for like the birds, about hidden treasure and the widow's mite (see Matt. 13:44-45; 6:19-34; Luke 12:22-34). But as we mentioned above, mammon is much more than money; and as we also noted in the 666 insights from the previous chapter, there are not one, but three paths of perversion that humanity might pursue. That, of course, included the wor$hip of big bucks, but was hardly the only voice of the trio.

A word of caution, however. When anyone presumes to rank sins from misdemeanors to mayhem on any kind of a numbering list, be it three to three thousand, there is a potential for this kind of thinking to lean toward legalism. The focus dare hardly be on three areas of sin, but rather our three areas of human response— by body, by soul, or by spirit. The Most High has a simpler way to sift out the saints than sorting their sins. There's really only one category of sin. Are we heading towards God or away from Him? Are we doing our utmost to bow before a King or to do a deal with a broker? This is the precise difference between a Hebraic highway and Greek shortcuts.

A simple insight to the Kingdom of God, therefore, is deeds versus direction. If the direction is right, the deeds will follow. But if it is performance that heads the parade—even though the deeds are good and proper—the direction could be anywhere but bowing before the Almighty.

Thus, there are two and only two choices for life that we can make and never the twain shall meet. This means that a seduction by a sort of subtle 21st-century polytheism (read: compromise of loyalties) can never be whitewashed over by any quick-fix claims of commitment. These include the public declarations we might make, the "religious" formalities we maintain, or any pious philosophies we pretend to follow. This may well signal the beginnings of a U-turn, but the end of it all must be the *purpose* we live for and the *mind-set* we live with—and die with.

Remember back in Chapter One when we first dropped by to check out Garden Tech College and we heard about the ongoing enrollment in Slithering Sam's Good and Evil Upgrade 101 class?

Perhaps we should go back and review these earlier chapters a bit more meaningfully. There were Plato's Divine Madness insights, and then Aristotle's apostasy in rejecting out of hand any nonhuman clues from the world beyond. There was the seduction of the

Sadducees, followed by not a few of the church fathers who fell in like fashion into a secularized fog. Then was the Darkest of Ages, including an eruption of unsettling anti-Semitism, followed by more of the same all the way into an Age of "enlightenment" of disappointingly low candlepower. Formal education soon degenerated to humanistic reprogramming the mind. Morality and principle began to unravel to the point that the UN affiliated Geneva Conventions were presumptuous enough to offer help with less than biblical Band-aids. Then finally we were able to tune into that new media talk show called "Mouth of the Beast." You got it. There's nothing new under the sun.

And that includes John the apostle's vision of the end of days in the Book of Revelation of which we have already had somewhat of an introduction in the previous chapter.

Therefore, the vision of the beast of netherworld beginnings that surfaced from the sea should still be fresh in your mind. He had horns of power; he had kingdoms of his territorial domain. And he had human protégées with lamb-like pretense following him, like so many puppets on a string, to promote a New World Order—without a doubt, no more orders from Abba! They want to show the Creator once for all that humanity has now come of age and can do it by themselves—and most likely, much better.

The last major flash of attention we shall see of this menacing monster—before things get a bit too hot for him to handle in the end of chapter 19 (see Rev. 19:19-21)—is in Revelation 17 where we have this red-robed mama of the street sitting on the beast's back, and who turns out to be not a little drunk at that. Let's check out her story.

> Then the angel carried me away in the Spirit into a desert. There I saw a woman sitting on a scarlet beast that was covered with blasphemous names and had seven heads and ten horns. The woman was dressed in purple and scarlet, and was glittering with gold, precious stones and pearls. She held a golden cup in her hand, filled with abominable

things and the filth of her adulteries. This title was written on her forehead:

MYSTERY

BABYLON THE GREAT

THE MOTHER OF PROSTITUTES

AND OF THE ABOMINATIONS OF THE EARTH.

I saw that the woman was drunk with the blood of the saints, the blood of those who bore testimony to Jesus... (Revelation 17:3-6).

Who in the world was she? Well, some of her closest friends might affectionately call her Baby Lonnie; but the Bible has named her Babylon, so we'll stick with that. Let's have another peek at a bit more of her bio.

The waters you saw, where the prostitute sits, are peoples, multitudes, nations and languages. The beast and the ten horns you saw will hate the prostitute. They will bring her to ruin and leave her naked; they will eat her flesh and burn her with fire. For God has put it in their hearts to accomplish His purpose by agreeing to give the beast their power to rule, until God's words are fulfilled. The woman you saw is that great city that rules over the kings of the earth (Revelation 17:15-18).

So from that added info, it becomes fairly clear who Baby Lonnie's real friends are. At the end of day, she doesn't have any. And even if she did, that sea-bourn beast and his ten-horned honchos would not be among them. When they're finished with her, they roast her alive, which is not at all uncharacteristic behavior of satan's little helpers, and all who follow him.

Now, the following chapter in Revelation, chapter 18, includes the translator's heading, *"The Fall of Babylon,"* which is the title used in most versions. To most Bible readers, this is a fairly well known end-of-days account of the final destruction of a "spiritual" Babylon. Following the 9-11 destruction of the World Trade Center, not a few seriously minded students of Scripture mentally flashed a direct connection with the Revelation 18 prophecy, reflecting upon what degree this chapter may or may not have with New York City, 11 September 2001.

Now, what many casual Bible readers of this *"Fall of Babylon"* chapter may *not* be as tuned into, is that this chapter of devastation and demise is *not* primarily for a physical city like The Big Apple (though we should never discount a secondary symbolism), but for the utter judgment, disgrace, and ruin of red-light Baby Lonnie herself. She opted for the best of both worlds, and when her own fortunes fell, she lost the lot!

Let's have just a bit of a look at chapter 18, to set the tone:

> *With a mighty voice [the angel] shouted: "Fallen! Fallen is Babylon the Great! She has become a home for demons and a haunt for every evil spirit...for all the nations have drunk the maddening wine of her adulteries. The kings of the earth committed adultery with her, and the merchants of the earth grew rich from her excessive luxuries"* (Revelation 18:2-3).

And then we hear another voice from Heaven:

> ...*"Come out of her, My people, so that you will not share in her sins, so that you will not receive any of her plagues; for her sins are piled up to heaven, and God has remembered her crimes"* (Revelation 18:4-5).

And one more window into her absolute annihilation:

> *"When the kings of the earth who committed adultery with her and shared her luxury see the smoke of her burning, they will weep and mourn over her. Terrified at her torment, they will stand far off and cry: 'Woe! Woe, O great city, O*

Babylon, city of power! In one hour your doom has come!"
(Revelation 18:9-10).

But for the original down-to-earth physical Babylon—which we have already credibly labeled, in Chapter Two, as the demonic capital of the globe—just happened to be the turf from which the Almighty pulled Abraham out of in order to start a flowing counter stream of Hebraic—*no other gods* before *Me*—monotheism.

The underlying principle behind that, of course, was that Babylon had traditionally represented the home of 1,031 flavors of pagan idolatry from the time of Nimrod until now. And as evil as Saddam Hussein and friends have been—and still are for that matter—they are not what make Babylon blasphemous. They just happened to like the place, and to tell the truth, they have fit in rather comfortably.[1]

So, let's tie this all together with that scarlet lady of lust who—in her initial introduction above—seems to be taking the joyride of her life on the spiny back of Beast bin Barnacles. But we must note with utmost attention that the sin of this infamous female was neither public drunkenness nor partying with promiscuous patrons behind closed doors. Rather, in exact Babylonian symbolism, her perversion as a prostitute can be nothing more or nothing less than the religious façade of "godlike" moral attachment, yet all the while, in and out of bed with either the *"kings of the earth"* or else the *"merchants"* of the same address (see Revelation 18:3).

Just to make sure that you get the connection, this is merely more of the same from that rival multiple-god kingdom that lives across the river on the other side of that Hellenist-Hebraic Great Divide. Since the Hellenists, as you know by now, have no problems with polytheism—catering to as many idols as suit their scenario—this creates a classic parallel for the prostitute who has no misgivings about multiple men. Her profits are merely proportional!

But don't forget, with Baby Lonnie, it's hardly just the men in her life. Focusing only on the flesh might let some of the heroes and heroines from Moral High Ground Village off a bit light. Remember, in addition to the flesh feature, those other two faces of mammon are big bucks and struggling for pole position in any and all facets of the human race-to-the-top-of-the-totem pole. Do I need to repeat that the recurrent big three from the Good Book, *"...the lust of the flesh, and the lust of the eyes, and the pride of life"* (1 John 2:15-16 KJV) are business as usual, mainstream events in the humanist mentality? Pledge your allegiance, say your prayers, and the rest of the day is yours to play with!

Something that the church in America and the rest of the West has never been able to get a handle on is that for some unknown reason—unknown to the Hellenist mind-set at least—the King of Creation likes limited loyalty far less than full-blown failure. And He makes it clear as He winds up the Good Book:

> *I know your deeds, that you are neither cold nor hot. I wish you were either one or the other! So, because you are luke-warm—neither hot nor cold—I am about to spit you out of my mouth. You say, "I am rich; I have acquired wealth and do not need a thing." But you do not realize that you are wretched, pitiful, poor, blind and naked. I counsel you to buy from Me gold refined in the fire, so you can become rich; and white clothes to wear, so you can cover your shameful nakedness; and salve to put on your eyes, so you can see* (Revelation 3:15-18).

So, who tells you when you're naked? There may be a myriad of means and messengers, but in the end of the day—God does!

And that's also why Abba is not all that happy about having His kids going across the river to Babylon for weekend diversions now and then.

ENDNOTE

1. Islam is presented as monotheistic by the media and secular world; however, many biblical scholars note pre sixth-century polytheistic origins, including association with Illat, the moon god of Arabic mythology.

CHAPTER FOURTEEN

ALL YOUR EGGS IN *HOW MANY* BASKETS?

NOW, we're getting into one last intriguing insight, so don't run off just yet. There are a few other clues interwoven into Baby Lonnie's global involvement that we should find even more revealing than her red and purple party dress.

In our first introduction to that demonically associated beast that surfaced from the sea back in chapter 12, we were told that one of his heads had *suffered from a deadly wound that had been healed* (see Rev. 13:3). This coded identity is mentioned twice more in the same chapter. Now, we have in the past heard some wild and wooly interpretations of this fatal-wound scenario. So, for the sake of credibility for any and all other serious concepts in this book, I find it best to not mention any of these here! Moreover, in 201,000 references on Google search, I haven't found one yet that gets anywhere near to what I'm going to suggest next. Okay, I haven't had time to hit all 201,000, but I did have a glance at quite a few. Mind you, I much prefer getting my directions from the Holy Writ and not from Google, but it's a bit interesting to find out if anyone else has ever tuned in on what I'm now going to tell you.

Some, unfortunately, have been tagging this deadly head wound—"beastly migraine" shall we call it—onto top-drawer religious personalities whose theology doesn't happen to match up with theirs. While yet others have laid the same presumptions on either popular or unpopular politicians who have passed on for some decades now, but who are expected back for either blessing or cursing as their political preferences may fantasize. Some of these "deadly wound" nominees, apostle John would never have dreamed of, let alone spoken out loud. So let's preferably proceed to Scripture for hopefully more realistic cross-reference clues.[1]

But for the moment, just keep in mind that we want to find out a bit more about this deadly wound that was healed. Keep it on the back burner because that's where we're heading, even though we first have to check up once more on what happened to Nimrod's original Babylon that made it as far in time as King Nebuchadnezzar's day.

First of all, in the Scriptures, there are prime predictions by two of the major Hebrew prophets, Isaiah and Jeremiah, describing in detail the physical annihilation of Ancient Babylon long before it happened. Here is a telling fragment of one such prophecy from chapter 21 of Isaiah:

> *Look, here comes a man in a chariot with a team of horses. And he gives back the answer: "Babylon has fallen, has fallen! All the images of its gods lie shattered on the ground!"* (Isaiah 21:9).

Chapters 50 and 51 of Jeremiah also provide a very accurate before-the-fact "report" on the fall of physical Babylon. In graphic imagery, Jeremiah prophesied in exact detail that Babylon was literally sunk. Seraiah, his staff officer, penned it out for him, and here are a few excerpts:

> *Jeremiah had written on a scroll about all the disasters that would come upon Babylon—all that had been recorded concerning Babylon. ..."O Lord, You have said You will destroy this place, so that neither man nor animal will live in it; it will be desolate forever." When you finish reading this scroll, tie a stone to it and throw it into the Euphrates. Then say,*

'So will Babylon sink to rise no more because of the disaster I will bring upon her..." (Jeremiah 51:60-64).

Ancient Babylon, or Babylon the Great, was indeed physically destroyed after the Persian invasion by Cyrus the Great in 538-9 B.C.

Of course, archaeologists know exactly where it was located, just south of Baghdad, and have dug up all kinds of ruins; but just as prophesied by God's prophets, the place truly has had it. But irony of ironies, just a few years back, Saddam Hussein was trying to patch some of it together for a national park. But as I'm sure you heard, he's recently been a bit more than occupied with other key commitments, and it's quite clear at this stage that this is one antiquity that is meant to stay that way. So even with die-hards like Saddam who have been eager—in more ways than one—to upstage the Word of God, Bible prophecy is still to be trusted. Babylon has pretty well had it!

However, there yet seems to be another small angle of confusion. Some 600 years after the fact, apostle John also gave us another foretold horrific destruction of a seemingly contrasting end-of-days Babylon in Revelation chapter 18. Remember, that was the glitzy city where Baby Lonnie lost everything her hungry heart had ever hoped for. And there were tears and such.

But hold on, if Babylon the Great had already been physically destroyed—totally wiped out—in 539 B.C., where in the world did this second end-of-days Baby Lonnie-Babylon come from?

Let's pick up the trail from where Babylon-II happened to hail from. We'll next investigate some cryptic clues from Revelation 17 where we have one of the heads of the beast—that is, a nation—that, *"...once was, now is not, and yet will come up out of the Abyss...."* Let's check out the full context:

> *Then the angel said to me: "Why are you astonished? I will explain to you the mystery of the woman and of the beast she rides, which has the seven heads and ten horns. The beast, which you saw, once was, now is not, and will come*

up out of the Abyss and go to his destruction. The inhabi-
tants of the earth whose names have not been written in the
book of life from the creation of the world will be astonished
when they see the beast, because he once was, now is not,
and yet will come (Revelation 17:7-8, emphasis added).

This sounds a bit fuzzy at first, so let's take it slow. Could this be in reference to the pagan, idolatrous, anti-God of the Bible, and anti-Jewish[2] Babylon the Great that had been overthrown some 600 years before John, and therefore back in his day, "now is not"? And yet again in our day, is it in the process of rebirth as an identical pagan, idolatrous, anti-God of the Bible, and anti-Jewish[3] One-World Government? Is this the New World Order now on line in the international think tanks and ready to roll? Anyway, lets wrap up our final clues to the cryptogram: In a second Revelation 17 text we have "seven kings, five are fallen." Again, let's have a look at the full context:

...The seven heads are seven hills on which the woman sits.
*They are also **seven kings. Five have fallen, one is, the***
other has not yet come; *but when he does come, he must*
remain for a little while. The beast who once was, and now
*is not, is **an eighth king**. He belongs to the seven and is*
going to his destruction (Revelation 17:9-11, emphasis
added).

In John's time, Babylon, Persia, Media, and Greece—four nations—had all been referred to by the prophet Daniel. And the fifth was undoubtedly Assyria, not mentioned by Daniel, but certainly a major player in Israel's history and the immediate predecessor of Babylon. The text goes on: *"...One is"* (that was Rome) and *"...one yet to come."* And once again, we have reference to a seventh kingdom in the sequence. (Daniel also refers to this end-of-days kingdom in Daniel 7:7, and again in a related context in Daniel 2:24-45.) Once more, this would appear to represent the presently emerging New World Order of Hellenist seed, as we see all Western politicians scrambling to establish their humanist, mammon-worshipping One-World government.

And what of the eighth king in that earlier text above? *"The beast who once was, and now is not, is an eighth king. He belongs to the seven and is going to his destruction."* Sure sounds like a repeat Scripture reinforcement to a resurrected "ideological" Babylon that is merely a synonym, a symbolic photocopy, or a new reflection of her ancient replica into the Hellenist-hatched New World Order.

Thus it appears that Babylon's deadly wound from the sword of Cyrus in 539 B.C. seems to have healed up quite nicely, and ready to go for one final round in the spiritual showdown with the Ancient of Days, the King of Creation, in our day and time.

And in summary, if anything has resuscitated that big, bad, pagan and multi-god Babylon back to life, it is the parallel Hellenistic humanism that we have waded through at every gully and every turn down the Garden path of Mrs. Adam's. Babylon is now no longer that physical city of idols, but a resurrected humanist "freedom" ideology of mix it or match it, replace it or patch it, or flavor it in any other way you fancy. Man is now in charge; the Most High has become an option for the aged at best, and for your last time to visit our particular mega-mall, "You are here!"

And that's what the prostitution of the scarlet lady is all about. Her clients are people, ordinary people with big appetites—or on occasion even teeny polite ones—for the best of both worlds.

That's what Hellenistic humanism is all about. It's about a different kind of freedom, a political term that has become quite popular in humanist circles these days. But lest anyone shortchange you on what it means, the fine print on their updated political kind of freedom means freedom from a disciplined lifestyle, freedom from responsibility, and especially—I hate to tell you—a freedom from an Abba-oriented relationship. And sadly, it doesn't mean freedom from a set of politicians—Western or otherwise—who are taking you places you really don't want to go.

And here's one more definition I don't want you to ever forget. Speaking of the significance of nakedness—nakedness in God's eyes is humanism that pretends to be dressed up!

On the other hand, Kingdom living is all about building into an intimacy-with-Abba relationship. It's all about mind-set. Why was I born? What am I here for? When all is said and done, who cares? For sure, I know that Abba does, and that He has those answers, not to mention all the others. And Kingdom living is all about intimate, personal communication with the King of the Universe. That's an option to get excited about!

I know you've heard since you were small never to keep all your eggs in one basket. Who told us that one? It's an "old wives' tale." Some of those old wives were pretty sharp they say. But others weren't. The one who came up with that multiple basket scenario, wasn't. She was Hellenistic, I might say.

Abba says, "One basket...Me alone."

And finally, in biblical circles, that's what the ever-expanding pursuit of our Hebraic roots in these days is all about. It's not about back to Moses, whom I reckon did a good job, and we know that his Abba appreciated it as well. But I like to go back further than that. I want to go back much further than getting all hung up on new legalisms; Emperor Constantine hoodwinked the church with enough of those to last a lifetime. And I like to go back even a lot further than Abraham whom the Almighty used to build His family of redemption. That was great, but I like to go all the way back to Abba who started the whole thing and who is still taking a few more enlistments.

I will rouse your sons, O Zion, against your sons, O Greece, and make you like a warrior's sword! (Zechariah 9:13b).

ENDNOTES

1. Adding to the several texts cited on this page, it is suggested that a reading of Isaiah 21, Jeremiah 50 and 51,

as well as the background chapters of Revelation 13, 17, and 18 will greatly enhance the insights presented.

2. Beyond symbolism of idolatry from the onset, Babylon's infamy with the Jewish people was her historic evil deed of destroying their sacred First Temple in 586 B.C., which mind-set has never changed over time.

3. Minimal research will reveal that a true "Jewish" State could never be tolerated in an avowed non-partisan New World Order. This explains current pressures upon Israel by Western powers (not to mention Islam) to cede Jewish land to the Arabs, which ultimately by demographic change or war would annihilate any God-fearing "remnant" in Israel. The Messianic reign of course, is the centrality of the biblical promise, and whether the Arabs and the "nations" accept it or reject it is beside the point. The bottom line is that anti-Semitism throughout Europe and the Middle East is endemic.

Contact and Resource Information

For international ministry schedules, requests for meetings, or books in English, Russian, Finnish, and Dutch by Victor Schlatter contact:

SOUTH PACIFIC ISLAND MINISTRIES, INC.

PO Box 990, Smithfield 4878, Qld. Australia

Fax: 07-4058-0258; International Fax: 617-4058-0258

E-mail: SpimAust@aol.com; info@spim.org.au

Visit our Website: http://www.spim.org.au

INTERNATIONAL BOOK SALES:

www.Amazon.com or www.barnesandnoble.com

BOOK SALES IN U.S.A.:

Destiny Image Publishers, Inc., PO Box 310,

Shippensburg, PA, 17257-0310 U.S.A.

Tel: 1-800-722-6774; Fax: 717-532-8646;or

E-mail: orders@destinyimage.com

AVAILABLE THROUGH ALL MAJOR CHRISTIAN BOOKSTORES.

Bulk sales for churches or non-profit organizations
(10 or more copies):
SPIM, Inc. Attention: Bernhard Laubli
Fax: 915-990-5525 E-mail: spimusa@mindspring.com

BOOK SALES IN AUSTRALIA:

Wholesale orders from:
W.A. Buchanan & Co., 37 Dalton St, Kippa Ring, 4021 Qld.
Tel: 07-3883-4022 Fax: 07-3883-4033
E-mail: service@wab.com.au

ALSO AVAILABLE FROM MAJOR CHRISTIAN BOOKSHOPS THROUGHOUT AUSTRALIA.

BOOK SALES IN ISRAEL:

The Galilee Experience, PO Box 1693, Tiberias 14115
Tel: 04-672-3260; E-mail: info@TheGalileeExperience.com

Emmanuel Messianic Bookshop
(Located adjacent to Christ Church)
PO Box 14037, Jaffa Gate, Old City, Jerusalem 911140
Tel: 02-627-7746; Fax: 02-626-3855;
E-mail: emb_shop@netvision.net.il

Kibbutz Ginosar Bookshop
Manager's Mob: 052-326-0990; Tel: 04 671-2073;
E-mail: mail@jesusboat.com

Qumran Visitors Center Book Dept.
Kibbutz Kalia: Tel: 02-993-6330;
E-mail: ordershop@kalia.org.il

Also available at ICEJ Bookshop; Vision for Israel;
Christian Friends of Israel; Bridges for Peace and most other
Christian support groups in Israel.

A BOOK WARNING OF ISLAMIC TERROR
THAT IRONICALLY HIT THE PRINTERS EXACTLY ON 9/11

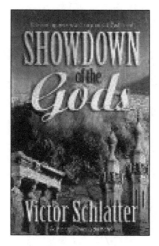

SHOWDOWN OF THE GODS

lays bare the two final challengers to the God of the Bible—Islam and a secular humanism long in germination for the occasion.

One day they feign friendship, the next day they kill each other-

The sub-title says it best:

THE EVENING NEWS
WON'T SURPRISE OLD ZECHARIAH!

"Victor Schlatter has again used his prophetic insight and voice to take on the global community of nations as far as their priorities are concerned. He did it previously in his book, Where is the Body? as he focused on the Church and Israel. But in Showdown of the Gods, Mr. Schlatter calls attention to the evil manipulations of nations in furthering their own interests. His own unique style adds a bit of humor to a very serious discussion of international priorities."

—George Giacumakis, PhD. Professor of History
California State University, Fullerton, CA.
Chairman of the Board, International Christian Embassy Jerusalem.

Full of facts and based on Bible Prophets...it opens your vision.

ORDER FROM:

Genesis Communications, Evergreen Press, 9350 Dauphin Island Parkway, Theodore, AL 36582 USA;Tel. 1.888.670.7463; Fax:251.973.0682; Email: info@evergreenpress.com

Amazon Books at: www.Amazon.com

South Pacific Island Ministries, PO 990, Smithfield, 4878 Qld, Australia; email: info@spim.org.au or SpimAust@aol.com
In USA: spimusa@mindspring.com

Or request from your local Christian Book Shop in Australia, USA, NZ, or UK.

SHOWDOWN OF THE GODS

UNIQUE IN APPROACH, SIMPLE IN
PRESENTATION, DEEP IN REALITY
165 Pages

"Where Is the Body?" is different. With the author's over 40 years of experience in the Third World, it was inspired and written with insights far more compatible with an original Middle Eastern setting and far less jaded with Twentieth Century trends and assumptions.

It is our wake-up call in these unpredictable days of Israel's preparation and testing. Its purpose is to jar the church into an awakening of what the God of Abraham is methodically setting up in Israel as groundwork for the return of His Son. It challenges not a few threadbare end-time assumptions such as have been given a ride on the coat tails of anti-Semitic thought latent in many segments of the Church. Its aim is to provoke honest thought, and above all, faithfully cites the Bible you say you believe.

"Where is the Body?" Is an Internationally Endorsed Release:

This is a fascinating and provocative book. Victor Schlatter exposes the anti-Semitism that so often distorts evangelical life and thought. He makes a strong case for a theology that centers on God's deep and abiding love for Israel and the Jewish people. I came away from reading his discussion with new insights of the Biblical message."

—Dr. Richard Mouw, PhD. Pres.
Fuller Theological Seminary, Pasadena, CA, USA

Forward: Rev. Malcolm Hedding, Director, ICEJ, Jerusalem.

Additional Endorsements: Clarence H. Wagner, Jr. International Director, Bridges for Peace, Jerusalem. **Dr. George Giacumakis, PhD**, Professor of History, Director, Mission Viejo Campus, California State Univ., Fullerton, CA. **Lance Lambert**, Prominent author, lecturer and authority on the history of Israel. Jerusalem, **Dr. Robert E. Cooley**, Chancellor, Gordon-Conwell Theological Seminary, So. Hamilton, MA, USA.

ORDER FROM:

Destiny Image Publishers, Inc.PO Box 310, Shippensburg, PA, 17257-0310 USA
Tel: 1.800.722.6774; Fax: (717) 532.8646;
or orders@destinyimage.com

Amazon Books at: www.Amazon.com

South Pacific Island Ministries, PO 990, Smithfield, 4878 Qld, Australia;
email: info@spim.org.au or SpimAust@aol.com
In USA: spimusa@mindspring.com

Or request from your local Christian Book Shop in Australia, USA, NZ, or UK.

For availability in Israel and additional details, see page 152.

TRANSLATED ALSO INTO RUSSIAN, FINNISH AND DUTCH

Additional copies of this book and other
book titles from DESTINY IMAGE are
available at your local bookstore.

Call toll free: 1-800-722-6774.

Send a request for a catalog to:

Destiny Image_® Publishers, Inc.

P.O. Box 310
Shippensburg, PA 17257-0310

*"Speaking to the Purposes of God for this
Generation and for the Generations to Come."*

For a complete list of our titles,
visit us at www.destinyimage.com